Contents

Introduction

Sir Linkalot says, 'What is linking?'

'In a **quarter** of an hour lesson, a **support** teacher **taught** me how to spell **nought** (zero).'

If you read this sentence to a group of young children, they would understand it, no problem. However, if you asked them to write it down, it's another matter altogether.

'Quarter', 'support', 'taught' and 'nought' all contain the same sound 'ort' but are spelled differently ... what chance have children got when they are learning to spell? Thanks to linking, every chance!

I do so love this English language of ours as it originates from all sorts of languages. The problem is, it doesn't half make spelling an issue! We can't have it both ways, I suppose.

There are techniques out there that can aid our spelling whether we are six or 66. Linking is one of these techniques but is being massively underused. It works for learning any fact, which I will illustrate later on. However, the primary focus in this book is helping Key Stage 1 and Key Stage 2 students with their literacy: in particular, spelling.

First things first, Sir Linkalot ... what is linking?

A person saying that they have a bad memory is a bit of a myth. We all have amazing memories, recalling vividly, for example, things that happened in our childhood. Your brain is designed to remember more facts and memories than you can possibly imagine. It's said that it permanently stores every single second of your waking life! Bonkers but apparently true. The trick is recalling these facts when you need to. This is where linking comes in.

Linking is a way of remembering a fact by creating a hook or a peg to hang the fact on, thereby making it easier to recall the fact at a later date. I like to call this hook or peg a link ... as it rhymes with think! We remember things better if it had a big impact at the time. For example, laughter, something visual or something clever that stimulates the brain tends to leave a bigger impression than most things. A strong link is one that makes you laugh, is clever or creates an unforgettable image.

Recalling facts by linking has been around for centuries but people haven't cottoned on to how useful it can be... until now that is!

Linking is basically another term for 'mnemonic' the official definition of which is: A device used as an aid in remembering.

Quite often when I ask people what a mnemonic is they automatically say it's a rhyme. This is not the case.

A link can be found in many shapes and sizes whether it be a catchy rhyme, an acronym or acrostic, a letter link (to be explained later), a picture, the use of famous people, number-play or a toe-curling cheesy pun (we all love them but tend to deny it).

I'm sure you've heard some of the following before:

Never **E**at **S**hredded **W**heat or **N**aughty **E**lephants **S**quirt **W**ater

This link helps you remember the compass points order.

Have you heard of these?

I ate and I ate until I was sick on the floor, eight eights are 64.

Red sky at night, shepherd's delight. Red sky in the morning, shepherd's warning.

i before e except after c. (Now don't get me started on that one!)

Big **e**lephants **c**an **a**lways **u**nderstand **s**mall **e**lephants - this helps with the spelling of 'because'.
(Elephants are getting far too much exposure in mnemonics as far as I'm concerned.)

Richard **o**f **Y**ork **g**ave **b**attle **i**n **v**ain (the initial letters of the colours of the rainbow).

Thinkalink!

The revolutionary spelling technique that will ensure your child can spell every word

Sir Linkalot

Thinkalink!

© Jade Creative Ltd

A catalogue record for this book is available from the British Library.

© Text: Andy Salmon

© Illustrations: Bill Stott

The right of Andy Salmon to be identified as author of this Work has been asserted by him in accordance with sections 77 and 78 of the Copyright, Designs and Patents Act 1988.

Thinkalink is a registered trademark of Andy Salmon.

Published by Jade Creative Ltd

Registered office: Manger House, 62a Highgate High Street, London, N6 5HX.

Registered number: 7940541.

Visit us online at www.theschoolrun.com for free printable activities, games and articles.

ISBN: 978-1-905096-90-9

There are 20 or 30 classics out in the ether somewhere but I felt linking shouldn't stop there. So, I have sadly/not so sadly (delete as necessary) been thinking of links for thousands of facts and it won't stop there! Here are a few spelling links to warm you up …

The **CIA** have spe**cia**l agents (this helps with the tough part of the word order in 'special').

U R A nat**ura**l speller (the 'u' of natural often gets omitted).

Runny, **r**unny, **h**elp … **o**ops! (this helps you spell the middle part of the word diarrhoea where letters are often missed or put in the wrong order. The visual link here helps keep the link in your head).

Some of these links will be lost on the weenies. They're for your benefit to illustrate how linking works, in general. However, there are hundreds of links that work for the five- and six-year-olds of this world, chiefly to do with spelling basic high-frequency words. Even better, these links can be used to remember words and facts throughout life.

Laws of Linking

1. Anyone can play.

2. It makes learning fun. The more fun you have, the easier it is to learn.

3. There is always more than one solution. Try and find your own connections because if it's meaningful to you, it'll stick better.

The aim of this book is to get the message across that, by employing linking at home, you can help your child enormously with their education. This book will concentrate on helping your child spell words from 'runny' to the far too graphical word above that doesn't need to be mentioned again.

The origin of Thinkalink

I contracted the linking lurgy whilst I was working in the money markets in 1995, an 'illness' I hasten to add that I have no desire of being cured of. At the time, my general knowledge was absolutely rubbish; all I was good for was maths and sport. But, like a lot of people, I have a fascination with maps.

One day, I was flicking through an atlas and saw that each state of America had a capital city which was news to ignorant ol' me. The first one I looked at was Ohio's capital, Columbus. My father introduced me to crosswords and puzzles when I was a nipper so I've always liked playing with words and enjoyed mental challenges. Consequently, being reasonably experienced with the construction of words, I put Ohio and Columbus in a memorable sentence to lock them together, thus…

Christopher **Columbus** never stops travelling … **'Oh, hi … oh**, he's gone, again!'

So thanks to the link, the next time I hear the state of Ohio mentioned, I will think of its capital, Columbus (or the other way round, of course).

I was now a linker and officially hooked.

I then linked the other 49 states, seeing it as a puzzle that I just had to solve, which I duly did. Linking is a game, after all. All that's required to play this game is a brain, an imagination and the ability to laugh a lot. We can all link as we all have an imagination. Some will pick it up straightaway whereas it will take time with others. It's a very powerful learning tool as we can all create our own link if we don't like the one we heard. It sure beats learning by rote, i.e. two and two is four, four and four is eight, eight and eight is 16 … two and two is four, four and four is eight, eight and eight is 16 … two and two is four … etc, etc, etc … zzz.

Having cut my teeth on state capitals, I then put aside my daily crossword challenge and proceeded to link like you wouldn't believe whenever I had a spare moment (it's a wonder that my wife is still with me!).

First up was the daunting task of the 200 or so world capitals (one of the top three most popular categories on the www.Thinkalink.co.uk website along with Spelling and Meaning of Words).

Here's one country-capital link that's stood the test of time …

Oman/Muscat. … **Oh man, I must cut** my hair!

Once I'd linked those, I had to move onto the next challenge. Appealing Pub Quiz categories seemed an obvious route to take ... Football Grounds, Best Film at the Oscars, Currencies, Christmas Number 1s, 12 Days of Christmas, James Bond (years *and* songs), 12 Apostles, 10 Commandments, Champagne Bottle Sizes (obviously), Airports, Time Zones, 12 Chinese New Years, American State Nicknames, Signs of the Zodiac, Olympic Venues and the Seven Wonders of the Ancient World. I felt that I had now earned my stripes and fully justified a place in the team for reasons other than just buying my 'superstar' teammates drinks all night.

This obsessive hobby continued with categories that were drifting into the educational world ... Bones of the Body, Greek & Roman Gods/Goddesses, British Prime Ministers, American Presidents, Battles & Wars, Kings and Queens, Historical Dates and the Periodic Table.

In 2005, it hit me that this was a tremendous learning tool for children to learn any fact that the teacher cared to throw at them. So, I got down to some serious linking business and worked on heavy-duty educational categories like Grammatical Errors, Word Meanings, Commonly Misspelled Words, French, Spanish, German and Latin Words, Times Tables, Science Formulae.

Having linked more than 10,000 facts in over 300 categories over a 10-year period, I now felt I was well equipped to tell the world about linking. So, in 2008, I sold my shares in the recruitment company I founded in 1998 and launched www.Thinkalink.co.uk which is a meeting place to learn a link for any fact or spelling you care to mention.

A big fat plus about the whole shooting-match of spelling and fact linking is that there's no right or wrong answer. If the link you've created works for you, then it works. It's great to think of your own links because then they are more meaningful to you thereby making them more memorable. It doesn't matter if your creation doesn't work for anyone else. If it does then that is the cherry on the cake!

There can be more than one answer. There could be, say, five links for the capital of Sweden, which is Stockholm and several links to remember the spelling of a single word. You might even create a fantastic spelling link to beat mine!

Spreading the joy of linking

Since the launch in 2008, Sir Linkalot (me!) has visited many schools, up and down the country, introducing thousands of children to the world of linking. This includes the weenies in Year 1 all the way up to the sixth form. I tend to spend the day there giving one hour workshops with each individual year. Included in these visits is an extra spelling session at the end of the day for those who would like to brush up on their spelling.

We have a lot of fun and laughter in these workshops as I challenge the children, individually and in groups to think of a link. The children come out of the workshop having got the message that linking is an extremely fun, interactive learning tool which they can put to use immediately to get their spelling in tip-top condition.

I insist that all teachers sit in on at least one of these sessions so they can grasp the techniques to put into use in everyday school life. Their participation is key as once I've gone it's vital that they keep spreading the joy. Just the same, it's important for you, as a parent, to understand how to link so you can help your child remember existing links while also creating their own.

Remember, have fun with linking!

Sir Linkalot

Sir Linkalot

Chapter One: The eight linking techniques

How do you think of a link?

Linking, like anything, takes practice. Some links will hit you straight on the chops in a heartbeat, others could take a while. I've had many years' practice and tend to use one of the eight techniques in this chapter when trying to *think* of a *link*.

This doesn't mean to say that you have to only apply these methods and these methods alone. When I set out on my linking journey, many moons ago, I was aware of only six of them. I stumbled across the other two - story linking and letter linking en route. What I love about linking is that it taps into everyone's imagination. You own your imagination so there are no rules to adhere to, no health and safety regulations and no terms or conditions.

The methods below work for me but may not necessarily work for you as our minds work differently. So, as the saying goes, one man's medicine is another man's poison. I am sure there are many other ways of remembering things but some of these eight should set you off in the right direction. I say 'some' as you don't need to restrict yourself to just one technique. The more methods you can use in a link the greater the impression it will leave. In the introduction of this book, the spelling of 'diarrhoea' uses techniques two, four and seven which are acrostics, visual and humour.

When you look at the methods, which are explained further on, don't feel the need to pick one and stick with that and, more importantly, don't dismiss one of the methods out of hand. The fact that you may not have used some of them to date doesn't mean that they won't work for you. Be open to all of them as some may grow on you. For example, initially I wasn't a fan of using acrostics. I feel they are massively overused which lessens their effect, thereby putting me off using them. I have now seen the light and realise that it is an extremely powerful technique when used correctly, i.e. diarrhoea, Never Eat Shredded Wheat, Richard of York ... etc.

On my travels, many children and teachers say that they are visual learners which may well be the case - pictures tend to be easier to recall than words. But that doesn't mean they should restrict themselves to just using images to remember things. Don't forget, our imaginations have no restrictions or parameters.

The beauty of linking is that I can't force a link to work on you but I can strongly urge you to be open to the eight methods below. I appreciate that some won't work for you initially but the more you try to use them the more chance you can think of a type of linking as your 'banker' or 'go to' method. I'm going to teach you some linking methods for facts as well as spelling linking, as the two go hand-in-hand.

1. Couplets (rhymes)

Using a two-line rhyme is a fun, but more importantly, very powerful way to remember something. The official term for this type of rhyme is a couplet.

Here's one to recall that Guy Fawkes' failed Gunpowder Plot was in 1605.

There was a BANG at the door at five past four (16.05)

16.05 is 4.05pm and a good back-up is that 05 is the 5th day in November.

If you are curious as to who Fawkes was trying to assassinate (King James I) then this couplet should light your fire...

King James the Scot didn't like flames a lot

The first of many warnings:

Make sure the couplet is short and snappy (a bit like the dwarf 'Grumpy'). Overuse of this excellent tried-and-tested technique lessens the impact. So use it wisely.

2. Acrostics

An acrostic (here's a simple visual link for an acrostic: a ✗ ✓) is where you make a sentence out of the first letter of each word in the sequence to make it more memorable. This is particularly useful in spelling or learning a sequence like the order of the planets.

Spelling example: The word 'future' can be misspelled in two or three different places. So this is where an acrostic comes into its own, as it includes every letter.

Freshen **up** **t**he **u**niverse. **R**ecycle **e**verything.

This technique is very often misused. It's crucial that you make it relevant.

For example: Freddie used the umbrella, readily, everyday ... is very forgettable as it has nothing to do with the word 'future' whereas the recycling message has.

Warning: Only use an acrostic for the tricky part of the word as the longer the acrostic, the harder it is to remember..

Here's an example of how a link works to remember sequences. Starting with the nearest to the Sun, the order of the planets are:

Mercury **V**enus **E**arth **Ma**rs **J**upiter **S**aturn **U**ranus **N**eptune

(Fact: Pluto has recently been demoted to being a humble dwarf planet so we're ignoring it. In case you wondered, it's the last planet.)

My **V**ery **E**normous **M**onster **J**ust **S**ucked **U**p **N**eptune

Note: Mercury and Mars could be mixed up. Just remember that 'my' and 'Mercury' begin and end with the same letters.

3. Famous people/things

Linking facts to a famous thing or person is a sure-fire way of remembering something.

Let's give you a couple of examples.

Chocolate, as wonderful as it is, is not an easy word to spell:

Cho**cola**te-flavoured Coca **Cola**? Gross!

US state Indiana is known as the Hoosier state.

Hey, **Indiana** Jones! Dr **Who's here** for you.

Staying with the doctor that little bit longer ...

The word **'wondrous'** is often spelt with a sneaky little vowel between the 'd' and 'r'.

The won**dr**ous **Dr** Who

Of course, if you haven't heard of Coca Cola or Dr Who then these links don't work!

4. Visual links

Many people are visual learners. When you have to remember the spelling of a word, you try and create a mental picture in your mind of the order but it's not easy. Throughout this book you will see some cartoons of visual links. A visual link can help commit the word to memory as pictures can sometimes be easier to remember than a specific order of letters.

For example, if you need to know how to spell 'eye', you have to learn four individual things, the 'e', the 'y', another 'e' and the order. This word is particularly tricky as you can't hear any of the three letters. With the image below, you only have to learn one thing, not four - the face where the eyes are drawn as an 'e' and the nose and mouth which are represented by a 'y'.

This is a powerful link as we are using a fact that the child already knows, here this is the order of the features on a face. Therefore they don't have to learn the order of the three letters *e, y* and *e*. A strong link means latching it onto information that a child already knows.

Let's look at another one.

The spelling of 'their' and 'there' are often mixed up, so a distinction has to be made.

Their: Belonging to them.

There: In or at that place

Their: The **'i'** is a person

There: The **'r'** is a signpost

You can bring to life anything you need to remember.

You've already seen a couplet for 1605 being the year of the Gunpowder Plot. However, you may prefer a visual link to commit it to memory. At one of my recent monthly school Thinkalink clubs, an 11-year-old girl created this link which I think is fab…

'There was a BANG (!) at the door at five past four (16.05)' - take your pick!

If you are a visual learner and you can think of a link then try and bring it to life by drawing your own cartoon. It will make it more memorable, especially if it's your own creation!

5. Story linking

I want to tell you a story …

The story line is the thread of a story which keeps it together very much like a link keeps together the thing(s) you need to learn. Putting a few facts into a short story is an excellent learning technique.

There are a lot of facts to remember here: 'The world's highest mountain is Mount Everest which is in the country of Nepal. It was first climbed by Sir Edmund Hillary and Sherpa Tenzing.'

Let's think of a link to remember these facts by creating a short story. Try saying it out loud:

'I need to **Everest** as my legs are **Tenzing** up and I've an **Nepal**ling stitch. This is a lot more **Hillary** than I first thought.'

6. Numbers

All ten numbers look like letters.

1 = I	2 = Z	3 = E (backwards)	4 = A	5 = S
6 = b or G	7 = j or y	8 = B	9 = g	0 = O

So bear this in mind when you need to remember a fact that contains the above letters. It's an extremely useful technique.

Session isn't the easiest word to spell. Using 1, 5 and 0, we get ...

5 + 5 = 10. That ends today's maths se**5510**n.

7. Humour (including puns)

Most people won't officially admit that they like bad jokes but often have a sneaky giggle on the quiet. A bad joke usually includes a play on words i.e. a pun - that rhymes with fun! William Shakespeare (aka Billy Waggledagger) was a pun-master. So who are we to argue with the Great Bard himself?

Something that makes you laugh tends to get automatically locked in the long-term memory bank. We all want to remember things that make us chuckle.

Prepare yourself for a couple of cheesy puns ...

French Words:

Horse/cheval - To scoop up a **horse**'s number twos, you use a **cheval**.

Chicken/poulet - Oi, Miss **Chicken**! Don't lay a **poo** ... **lay** an egg! (Sorry.)

It's all good pun.

8. Letter linking

To say that I am hugely pumped about the prospect of telling you how fantastic this underused learning technique is would be a gross understatement. It is making a serious dent in children's spelling issues, regardless of age and ability. I appreciate that this is a bold statement and then some, but it's not unfounded.

More often than not, there is just one tricky letter which makes people misspell a word. This is good news, as the fewer letters that are the issue, the easier it is to link.

Letter linking is using a familiar expression to help you spell a word.

This is the formula:

(Tricky word to spell) + (easier word to spell) + (expression) = tricky word spelled correctly!

Children know thousands of facts and expressions. Let's get them to use these to help them learn other things, rather than making up a new mnemonic which they need to learn as well!

Let's give you a couple of examples.

The '**w**' of '**w**rist', the '**g**' of **g**nome and the '**b**' of 'com**b**' are all silent letters. We need a *letter link* to remind you of this.

Wrap: **w**rap up **w**arm   **Crumb:** **b**readcrum**b**   **Write:** **w**rite **w**ords

See how the first letter of the second word 'warm' reminds you of the letter 'w' in 'wrap'.

There's no limit to letter linking. This technique can also work for multiple letters.

Biscuit: Cup of tea and a bis**cui**t ... or ... **cu**stard cream bis**cui**t.

Surprise: Burp! That s**urp**rised me.

Exaggerate: You need to ex**agger**ate to st**agger** me.

So if you can spell 'cup', 'burp' and 'stagger' then you can spell 'biscuit', 'surprise' and 'exaggerate'. If you can't spell 'cup', 'burp' or 'stagger' then we need to think of links for those first. When it comes to applying linking to spelling, start with the small basic words then work up to the biggies when the time is right. One step at a time...

I'll be explaining this oh-so-fabby technique in a lot more detail in the next chapter for oodles of words useful for Year 1 and up.

I make no apology for repeating myself but I can't tell you how useful it is for spelling.

In fact, let's do a quick exercise which you can try with your child. Once you've explained the *letter linking* technique, ask them if they can think of a *letter link* (or two) for the following words...

(I've highlighted the tricky letter which needs to be the first letter of another word.)

Let's look at 'chef' first.

The way to phrase it is:

'What do chefs do?'

And the link is: **c**hefs **c**ook.

Your turn!

De**s**ert:

Wrong:

Whole:

Knife:

(Suggested answers are at the end of this chapter. Have a go before you have a peek.)

Letter linking can also help you with other facts to learn, in particular the meaning of words. If you can match a big chunk of the word that you need to learn with an easier word that has a similar meaning, then you're off to the races!

For example:

Utilise means 'to use'.

Covert means 'hidden' or 'secret' (a covert operation in the army).

Frail means 'fragile'.

Purge means 'to make pure' or 'cleanse' (to purge your body or soul).

Culpable means 'guilty' or 'deserving of blame'.

These words might not apply to the younger children just yet. They're just to illustrate the diversity of *letter linking*.

With the first four here – covert and purge - take a look inside and see what can be revealed.

With the last one, can you think of a word that begins with 'culp' that has something to do with 'guilty' or 'deserving of blame'?

Hopefully you have come up with the following:

Utili**se**: use.

Covert: cover (if you cover something it's hidden or secret).

Frail: **fragi**le.

Purge: pure.

Culpable: **culp**rit.

All the handful of words in the dictionary that begin 'culp' mean 'blameworthy'. They derive from the Latin 'culpa' which means 'blame'. So linking is very useful to show you where words originate.

Suggested answers for the five letter links on page 13

Desert sand   **Desert sun**   **S**ahara de**s**ert

Wrong **w**ay.

Whole **w**orld.

Kitchen **k**nife.

It doesn't matter if they can't spell the corresponding word i.e. Sahara, World or Kitchen. All they need to know is the first letter. We can think of links for the rest of the word separately.

Chapter Two: Spelling techniques

Why spelling is important

I recently read in a national newspaper that 46% of people judge you negatively if you are a weak speller. Linking won't necessarily bring that percentage down but what it will hopefully do is exclude your child from that bracket.

It does help enormously that we are in the world of the 'spellcheque' (sorry, couldn't resist it). It's extremely reliable but does throw you once in a while, as it struggles to shake off its American roots. Plus there is the added problem that you might spell a word correctly, but it is in the wrong context; this is especially important when it comes to homophones such as 'there' and 'their' or 'you're' and 'your'. The spellcheck thinks it is right, but a reader will know it isn't. That's why you still need to know how to spell even when using a computer.

Some incredible pre-technology 'movers and shakers' had serious learning difficulties but they stuck with it and succeeded in their field. These days, children who struggle with their spelling are allowed to use computers in class – an excellent idea. The last thing you want to do is crush a child's spirit due to a learning difference they may have. Technology is a wonderful thing and should be embraced when it comes to education.

Going back to that stat, it means that one in every two people who interview you for a job will turn you down if you're spelling is an issue. (Test: do you see what is wrong with that last sentence? Yes, the computer thought 'you're' was okay as it is spelled correctly but it's actually wrong here - 'your' is the correct spelling.) Ironically, the main reason for this is due to the above statistic, i.e. they are worried that one in every two clients will judge the company on a representative's weak spelling, thereby missing out on potential business. So the interviewer's decision is not a reflection on your ability but more what is perceived to be your ability. Someone once said to me that perception is reality, which is a very interesting observation.

But before you go for a job interview, you have to first get the interview, which your exam results will have a huge impact on. Just to stay on my soap box that little bit longer... all exam results do is get you the interview, they don't get you the job. Who you are gets you the job. After 10 years of running a recruitment company, I believe that a person with confidence has a greater chance of getting a job than someone who doesn't. Linking instils that confidence. If you have the confidence to learn then you will learn.

Spelling is the first thing you learn when you're a nipper. Once you're on top of that, you can then read which enables you to learn what words mean, consequently permitting you to understand things. Once you understand, you can then form an opinion which in turn helps to form your character. You are now ready to conquer the world!

What spelling techniques are currently out there?

1. A word inside a word

Finding a word inside another word is, firstly, an enjoyable game and, secondly, an extremely useful way to aid your spelling. This technique has been around since the year dot but is not being used to its full potential.

a) Ask your child what small words they can unearth in the following bunch of hot potatoes that are often misspelled:

Hint: Ask them to try and include the tricky letter in the word they find.

It doesn't matter if some of these words are beyond your child. They would have heard of most of the words inside that are used for the link. So they can still play. It will get them used to this technique which they can apply to less difficult words. I've done the first one for you:

White

Flood   Orange   Soldier   Believe   Vegetable

b) These five have two words hidden away together. See if you child can spot them:

Salad   Theme   Nuisance   Machine   Meant

c) The following four have words in them that are backwards.

Hint: One of them uses every letter of the word!

Wednesday   Recipe   Stressed   Receipt

It doesn't matter if the word you have spied is backwards. Your brain will store a little reminder in its memory bank that there is a word inside another word. You will work out very quickly whether it's forwards and backwards.

Answers

How did they get on?

Here are the answers (there could, in some cases, be more than one correct answer):

a) One word in another word

White   **Fl**oo**d**   **Or**ang**e**   Sol**die**r   Be**lie**ve   Ve**get**able

b) Two words in another word

S **a lad**   **The me**   Nu **is a** nce   M **a chin** e   **Me ant**

c) A word in another word, backwards

We**dnes**day   Re**cipe**   **Stressed**   **Receip**t

Once you've found the word, you are three-quarters of the way there. All you need to do is put them into a sentence to make it snappy. Give it a go.

Here are some suggestions for you to salute or to give the boot:

a) One word in another word

White   Flood   Orange   Soldier   Believe   Vegetable

I **hit** a w**hit**e golf ball

Don't f**loo**d the **loo**!

My O**rang**e mobile phone just **rang**.

Sol**die**rs **die** in battle

This is one **lie** you have to be**lie**ve.

Go and **get** the ve**geT**ABLEs and put them on the TABLE!

b) Two words in a word

Salad   Theme   Nuisance   Machine   Meant

A lad should eat **s**alad

The theme today is '**me**'!

Nu**isa**nce **is a** nuisance to spell.

A chin-up for my friend is a breeze … he's a m**achin**e!

'**Me** and **Ant** are **meant** to be together,' says Dec.

c) A word in another word, backwards

Wednesday   Recipe   Stressed   Receipt

Send (**dnes** backwards) it on We**dnes**day

That re**cipe** was an epic! (**cipe** backwards)

We're stressed (**desserts** backwards) as our **desserts** haven't arrived!

Is this piece (**eceip** backwards) of paper the **receip**t?

Oi! Break it up, break it up...

Trying to find words that are purely made up of other smaller words is firstly a hoot and secondly a very useful spelling technique.

Medallion: Medal Lion   **Repertoire**: Re Per To I Re   **Patisseries**: Pat Is Series

2. Letter representation

This is an extremely useful technique where letters can represent something else.

I'm sure there are many more but take a peek at these...

aa – AA batteries, Automobile Association

ae – Accident & Emergency (A&E)

ai – A1 (something that is excellent is called A1) AI (Artificial Intelligence)

ant – Ant & Dec

bb – Bed & Breakfast, Big Brother

cc – 1000cc bike, Closed-circuit TV (CCTV), To see (2C), Carbon copy (as in 'cc an email')

cia – Central Intelligence Agency (CIA)

cid – Criminal Investigation Department (CID)

dd – Donald Duck

dec – December, Ant & Dec

dr – Doctor

e – email, E numbers

ec – European Community

eco – Eco-warrior

er – Emergency Room (ER)

et – ET (Extra-Terrestrial!)

eu – European Union

ew – East to West

gu – Gü (scrummy chocolate pudding brand)

gui – GUI i.e computer mouse (Graphic User Interface)

h – Hospital

ici – One of the world's biggest companies

io – 10 (ten)

ist – 1st (first)

ll – Railway tracks, a road, a pair of legs, a ladder, 'to hell' (2 L), the number eleven

mis – MI5 (The UK's secret service)

mm – M&Ms, Millimetres, Mickey Mouse, Eminem, This Millennium (MM)

ne – North East

nn – Dublin (Double N)

oi! – Trying to get someone's attention

oo – O2 Arena, double zero, Pair of eyes, Pair of cheeks, Pair of wheels

ou – Owe you; Oh, you

ow! – A cry of pain

pp – Postage & Packing (P&P)

rio – Rio Ferdinand (footballer), Rio de Janeiro (Brazil)

rr – Rolls Royce, Rest & Relaxation (R&R), Rock & Roll (R&R)

se – South East

ss – Secret Service

st – Saint

ugh! – An expression when something's gone horribly wrong

uk – United Kingdom

So if you needed to remember that there is a double 'm' in 'swimming' then use one of the abbreviations. The idea is that you can use these well-known letter representations to create links, for example:

a) **M&M**s are swi**mm**ing in calories

b) Swi**mm**ing races are often decided by millimetres (**mm**)

c) The facilities at this swi**mm**ing pool are Mickey Mouse (**mm**)

d) Do you listen to **Eminem (M&M)** when you're swi**mm**ing?

Take your pick or, better still, create your own!

Here are a few more examples:

Look: You l**oo**k with your eyes (**o o**)

Blew: The wind b**lew** from **E**ast to **W**est

Br**eakfa**st: I need br**eakfa**st to charge my personal **AA** batteries.

Illegal: It's i**ll**egal to park on double yellow lines (**ll**).

Station**ery**: **E**-mail is killing off station**ery**. Or the word **toner** is in sta**tioner**y

Archaeologist: **Archae**olog**i**st Indiana Jones' **arch** rival ended up in **A&E** having been hit by a **log**.

Looking at the last example, you can see that three little gems have been unearthed. It's amazing what you can discover in a word to aid its spelling.

Now you can spell 'look', you can extend this to help you spell other words that have 'oo' in them by putting them into a familiar sentence:

I t**oo**k a l**oo**k at the c**oo**k b**oo**k.

There are oodles more words with 'oo' in them. Get your child to use this technique to help them spell some of them

Double letters in a word can be a problem as they usually make the same sound as a single letter. Here are four examples ...

Di**sapp**oint   Di**sapp**ear   Emba**rra**ss   A**nn**iversary

... and here are four suggested links ...

2P or not **2P**? That **S** the question.

Shakespeare never di**sapp**oints and will never di**sapp**ear.

That's doubly emba**rra**ssing, mum!

My parents are off to **Double N** (Dublin) for their wedding a**nn**iversary.

The **CIA** are spe**cia**l, Mr Bond.

Did you know that all words ending -cian are jobs?

Here are a selection of jobs that all end with -cian:

Beauti**cia**n   Dieti**cia**n   Electri**cia**n   Magi**cia**n   Mathemati**cia**n

Musi**cia**n   Opti**cia**n   Politi**cia**n   Physi**cia**n   Techni**cia**n

The American version of James Bond works for the CIA (Central Intelligence Agency).

The above people work for a company and have a company (the CIA) inside their name!

The **CIA** are spe**cia**l as it's in the wording.

If you haven't heard of the **CIA** just remember that it's a **C**ompany **I**n **A**merica.

As you can see, letters often represent something in everyday life which is good news. The easiest links to recall are the ones we can immediately relate to.

3. Text language

R. I C Y U Q 4 T ... 2 B Polite!

Some letters and numbers make the same sound as words which can be extremely useful when linking. The following have been used over the centuries (IOU, for example) but have recently come into their own since the emergence of text messaging.

B = Be/Bee   C = See/Sea   I = Eye/Aye   Q = Cue/Queue

R = Are/Ah   T = Tea/Tee   U = You/Ewe   Y = Why

1 = Won   2 = To/Too   4 = For/Fore   8 = Ate/Hate

Get your child to play with them to think of links for the spelling of these little pixies:

Cour**se**   Fr**ui**t J**uice**   Su**cce**ss   Feb**rua**ry   **Out**

Close Ur Is B4 U C my suggestions. I 1der if **U R A** nat**ura**l linker?

Of course **U R**!

U and **I** ought to drink fr**ui**t j**uic**e as it has lots of vitamin **C**.

It's great **2 C** su**cc**ess.

R U A sucker for Valentine's in Feb**rua**ry?

Oi, **U** ... o**ut**!

Now your child can hopefully spell 'out' just as they can spell 'look'. Ask them to put it into a familiar sentence to help them spell some other words that contain 'ou'.

Here are two examples:

1. Out, Loud, You & Shout

Here is a suggestion ... **Y**o**u** sh**out** o**ut** l**ou**d.

2. Out, Found, Around, About, Four, Pound & Sound

'I've just fo**u**nd **out** that I **O U** ar**ou**nd ab**out** f**ou**r p**ou**nd' ... 'S**ou**nd!'

'Colour' is often misspelled as the sound of the word is nothing like its spelling.

a) What c**ol**o**ur** are **ur** eyes? (**o o**)

b) The c**ol**o**ur** of **ur** cheeks (**o o**)

Here I've combined the letter representation technique with text language which can only enhance the link.

Text language has been around for many years ... 'IOU' is a classic. Some people balk at this language but I embrace it. Children (and adults!) are forever using it to communicate, so we may as well use it to our advantage.

Breaking the law

There are many rules in the English language but there is always an exception to the rule.

Take this one, for example: **i** before **e** except after **c** (br**ief** and rec**ei**ve)

It's a catchy link as it has used rhyme linking. Unfortunately, as it stands, there are many exceptions.

Also, who's to say it is 'belief and receive' not 'beleef and receeve'?

The rule should really be:

i before e except after c, as long as it's pronounced as a long e and you know it contains an i

This is becoming too much of a mouthful and therefore has less chance of being committed to memory. You also have to explain what a long e is (pronounced 'ee'). This defeats the object of a memory-aid and what it stands for. Even if you do manage to remember this extended rule, there are still a few exceptions. The solution is to *think* of a *link* for each individual word.

'S**ei**ze' and '**weird**' are two of them that live outside the letter of the law.

a) Sei**ze** the pri**ze**

b) That b**ird** looks we**ird**.

c) The 'i before e' rule doesn't apply here. How w**ei**rd.

Some of the above links for 'seize' and 'weird' used the technique *letter linking* - where you *link* the *letter(s)* that's troubling you with the same letter(s) in another word in a familiar expression.

Your brain has stored away many thousands of expressions (yes, many thousands!) and you can recall virtually all of them. Things like 'bread and butter', 'pull your trousers up', 'join in', 'football pitch', 'remote control'.

So we must make the most of this amazing fact when it comes to spelling.

4. Letter linking gets you thinking!

Some of the above links for 'seize' and 'weird' used the technique letter linking. Let's recap the formula for letter linking:

(Tricky word to spell) + (easier word to spell) + (expression) = tricky word spelled!

Attaching the word you need to spell to one of the many thousands of expressions that is already stored in the grey matter saves you having to learn a new mnemonic.

See if your child can *letter link* these words:

(The awkward letters are highlighted.)

Com**b**
Ob**e**y

Swe**a**t
Lon**d**on

Ne**cess**ary
Inte**rr**upt

Tip:
You don't need to just link the bold letters. You can add the letters either side to make it easier. Note that the letters don't have to be together for it to work, e.g. Lon**d**on

As always with linking, there's more than one answer. Here's what I've come up with ...

Brush and com**b**
Obe**y** and **be**have

Armpits swe**at**
Lond**on** **Z**oo

It's ne**cess**ary to listen in **class**
Uncle **Terr**y's won a Medi**terr**anean cruise!

That's just bang out of order!

As you an now see, the letters don't have to be in order for *letter linking* to work. As long as you know that the letters appear somewhere in the word then all is tickety-boo as common sense takes over.

Here are two examples ...

1. O**ccu**r

Cra**c**ks o**cc**ur in old age

2. O**cc**asion

The **socc**er World Cup is a huge o**cc**asion (the first o is a football)

My personal best for the longest *letter link* is six letters. See if you can beat it.

It's for knowing how many of the letters 'c' and 'm' there are in the word 'recommend'.

I re**commen**d you read my **commen**ts in your school report.

Here are two more that may work...

PE teachers re**comm**end you go for a run on the **comm**on.

I re**comm**end you use **comm**as and full stops.

If you aren't sure how many Ms there are in comment, common or comma then think of links for these first. There are a dozen dos and don'ts in Chapter Four that offer some helpful tips.

How the internet can help when letter linking

Using 'pla**c**id' and 'o**pport**unity' as two examples, go online and type in a search engine (or look in a dictionary) ...

a) Definition of placid

When you find a dictionary site, scroll down to find the definition for 'placid' and look for words that are related to it that have a '**c**' in them somewhere, ideally at the start. This is where I found '**c**alm'. Do note that this won't always come up trumps but it's been extremely useful for me.

b) Words containing 'pport'

There are sites that list words containing any combination of letters you want. When you are in one of these sites, look at the list of words that have 'pport' in them that you can somehow link to the word 'opportunity'. I found 'support' and duly linked it.

I'll su**pport** you at every o**pport**unity.

This is an excellent way of using the internet to help you learn.

Letter linking is very much like spotting a word in another word but in this case it's only part of the word. You will have the common sense to drop the letter that is clearly not in the word, i.e. the 'y' of '**Terr**y' in 'in**terr**upt'.

You scratch my back ...

As we know, the trick is to use as many expressions as possible when trying to think of a link. The next technique is an extension of *letter linking* which I have called *double letter linking*. It's where two tricky words in a familiar expression can help each other ... in other words, you scratch my back and I'll scratch yours.

For instance: You can't hear the **e** of h**e**art and the *a* of be**a**t

So, if you just remember the expression 'h**e**artb**ea**t', you'll be able to know how to spell both 'heart' and 'beat'.

The 'a' sound in 'heart' reminds you that there is an 'a' in 'beat'.

The 'e' sound in 'beat' reminds you that there is an 'e' in 'heart'.

Here are some more examples:

'**He**ad**ach**e' (You can't hear the '**a**' of 'he**a**d' and the '**h**' of 'ac**h**e'.)

'**He**alth and safety' (You can't hear the '**a**' of 'he**a**lth' and the '**e**' of 'sa**fe**ty'.)

'**Yo**ung and **You**th' (You can't hear the '**o**' of 'y**o**ung' and the '**u**' of 'yo**u**th'.)

'**Wh**y and **Wh**o' – '**Wh**y call him Dr **Wh**o?' (You can't hear the '**h**' of 'w**h**y' and the '**w**' of 'w**h**o'.)

Letter linking in all its many guises is a joy as you can apply it to hundreds of words and it's a very gentle introduction to linking.

These are a few techniques that I have found very useful when trying to make spelling easier and more fun. There could well be more methods out there. At the end of this book, I've included information on how you can submit your links to the www.Thinkalink.co.uk website.

Let's practise linking!

1. Ask your child to try and spell a word that you have selected from your own list.

2. If they misspell it, make a note of which letters they get wrong.

3. Go to Chapter Four and look up the word you want a spelling link for.

(If the word isn't there, go to www.thinkalink.co.uk and request a link for it.)

4. Make a note of which of the following three categories the link falls under and put it up your sleeve, so to speak:

a) **WW: W**ord inside another **W**ord.

b) **LR: L**etter **R**epresentation ('oo' is a pair of eyes, for example.)

c) **LL: L**etter **L**ink (part-word inside another word).

5. a) If it's a **WW**, ask them if they can see the word that's inside.

b) If it's an **LR**, ask them if they can spot it.

c) If it's an **LL**, ask them to try and think of another word that is naturally linked to it which contains the letter they had a problem with.

Need some examples?

1. Words inside words (WW)

Ask them to see what words they can spot inside the following three words:

a) Eat

b) Huge

c) Parent

Once they have discovered them (aided or unaided), ask them to put the two words in an expression or short, catchy sentence thereby creating a link. Get them to write the link next to the word in question. (Suggestions are at the end of this section.)

2. Letter representation (LR)

I have put what the highlighted letters represent next to each word.

a) No**se**   **SE** = South East

b) Marve**ll**ous   **ll** = Pair of legs

c) Confection**e**ry   **E** = E number

Ask your child to try and put the word and the LR into a short sentence. (Suggested answers are at the end of this section.)

3. Letter links (LL)

I've highlighted the bits that are commonly misspelled in the following three words:

a) Anc**ho**r

b) Lam**b**

c) W**o**rk

Ask them to think of words that are found in a common expression which contain the awkward letters.

Suggested Answers

1. WW

a) Eat: **E**at **at** the table

b) Huge: A **hug**e **hug**

c) Parent: **Pa**re**n**ts **are** always right!

2. LR

a) Nose: A no**se** points **s**outh **e**ast

b) Marvellous   A marve**ll**ous pair of legs (**ll**)

c) Confectionery: Confection**ery** can contain **E** numbers

3. LL

a) Anchor: The **ho**ok of an anc**ho**r

b) Lamb: A lam**b** says '**B**aa'!

c) Work: **Ho**mew**or**k

Chapter Three: Practical tips for parents and teachers

'Whether on an individual basis or in a group session, I have taken exactly the same approach to every child I have presented linking techniques to, regardless of age and ability... yes, exactly the same.'

Can anyone use linking techniques?

As we've discovered, linking is attaching the thing or word the child needs to learn to something that is already in their memory bank. So, regardless of the learning difference the child has – dyslexia, dyspraxia, dyscalculia, dysgraphia, Asperger's, ADHD, ADD, autism etc – they have either heard of the expression 'cup of tea and a biscuit' or not. If they haven't, then the link won't work. Therefore, there are no separate approaches to take depending on your child's requirements.

As we know in teaching, whether as a parent or as a teacher, engaging the child is half the battle. When they have to learn something new they fear that they may not understand or remember it. But if you say to them from the onset that we are going to be using familiar expressions to help them learn, not new stuff, then there is a much greater chance of engaging them.

In this chapter I mention dyslexia a few times as misspelling is a common symptom but I'm fully aware that spelling is a symptom of other learning differences. The techniques still apply to all.

Linking works for any fact that a child needs to learn whether it's for the spelling of 'comb' or the group classifications of elements in the Periodic Table! However, in this book we have concentrated on spelling.

This is helping children of all ages and ability enormously with their literacy. Since I launched www. Thinkalink.co.uk in May 2008, I have conducted regular classes (group and individual) for local children and adults who have spelling difficulties including many with dyslexia. These classes have been a source of great amusement for my students but, more importantly, extremely constructive. The strength of linking is that it empowers the person so they can go away and think of links for whatever they need to learn. I set them challenges in the session and give them homework. This can take many forms but a good chunk of it is *letter linking*.

This is not a cure for dyslexia but it is putting a huge dent in spelling issues.

One of the problems with dyslexia is that people often see letters and numbers in a different order, which is a real stumbling block. Linking tries to get away from what is written down on paper by expressing it in a different way using some information that the person already knows.

It's already been mentioned in this book that the spelling of 'biscuit' is a classic example.

If you sound out 'biscuit', you get: bis-q-it.... or ... bis-qu-it ... or ... bis-koo-it ... etc.

It's too random.

Concentrate on the tricky bit '**cu**' and ask the child if they can think of an expression that has 'bis**cu**it' in it plus another word beginning '**cu**'. There are various possibilities but '**cu**p of tea and a bis**cu**it' works well (or milk/juice/water). If the child can't spell 'cup' then you think of a link for that before moving on. For example, 'the handle of a **c**up is **c**-shaped'.

By doing it this way, you're getting the child to join in by hopefully creating their own link. They are far less likely to forget their own creation than someone else's.

Where to begin

You will see a section later on in the book which includes links for lots of high-frequency words categorised by number of letters, starting with two, three, four letters and so on.

Depending on age and ability, start with the tiny words and work your way up.

I would suggest picking out, say, 10 words that are on your child's class list to learn. Look at the suggested links for each one before the lesson/session which you can then keep up your sleeve. If you can think of your own links for any of these 10 then all the better! You should now be well-equipped for the lesson.

If you are teaching a class then split the children into small groups. This is a good idea for three reasons.

1. They can bounce ideas off each other sharing their thoughts and creations.

2. It's great for team bonding.

3. It creates healthy competition in the classroom.

You then hand out the 10 words you want letter links for, underlining the tricky letter(s). For example:

S**o**n   De**a**d   Crum**b**   **C**hef   Bom**b**

Coat   Ha**u**l   **B**ath   E**asy**   **Tw**o

Ask them to put the highlighted letters in another word that has some natural link with the word in question.

Give the kids a few minutes to see what they come out with and encourage them to draw a link if it's a visual one. For example, drawing a smiley face in the '**o**' of 's**o**n' is a good idea. It will remind them that there is a boy's face in the word 'son' as opposed to 'sun'.

You can put your own stamp on this task. For example, putting the children into teams with the clock ticking is always a hoot. Get them to vote on each link giving it a mark out of 10. The link with the lowest score isn't a loser as it obviously worked for the one who created it. Everyone's a winner!

Here are some links which should do the trick:

S**o**n and b**oy**   De**a**d or **a**live   **B**readcrum**b**   **C**hefs **c**ook
A bom**b** goes '**b**ang'!

Hat and coat   Ha**u**l **u**p   **B**ath mat   E**asy** **as** that
Twins are **tw**o people

It doesn't matter that they can't spell 'alive' or 'bread'. All they need to know is the first letter. We can think of a link for these words at some other stage.

The same theory applies for tougher words. So it can apply to any year group. You might even find yourself using links for commonly misspelled words.

Sorry to sound like a scratched record but the great thing about linking is there is more than one answer. So, if the child can think of a link that works for them, then it works! As there is never a wrong answer it will encourage other children to give it a go, including the shy ones or those who lack confidence.

The best way forward

The ideal way to put this into practice is to look up a link from the list in Chapter Four for a word the child needs help with and have it ready up your sleeve. Then ask your child to see if they can think of a link for the awkward part of the word.

If they struggle, depending on what technique was used, ask:

Can they see a word inside a word even if it's backwards?
Do the tricky letter(s) represent something else? (Letter representation.)
Can they think of a letter link for the tough bit?
Are the difficult letters used in text language at all? (i, o, u, c, r, b ... etc.)
Can they create an acrostic? (This is not a 'go to' technique. Use sparingly.)

The art of teaching is to feed the student bit by bit until they can feed themselves. It works for all ages and ability. Some will grasp it immediately; others will take a tad longer. The exciting thing is that there is a solution to their spelling issues, assuming the person can spell phonetically. If they can't then it will work, but it'll be a far longer journey.

Interestingly, I have found that children who can't commit something to memory on first hearing or reading make good linkers as they have had to think laterally to remember things to date. So they have already used their imagination to learn.

I have taught many children who have dyslexia and ADHD, for example, and they have come up with tremendous links for all kinds of stuff. Many of the autistic children I have worked with have incredible brains and can remember facts at will. The problem they have is that they have trouble communicating these thoughts in a social situation. Linking crosses this barrier as they can think of outstanding links which they share with their peers via me. The cherry on the cake is that it gives them something to be proud of.

Linking instils confidence, regardless of age and ability.

All I am doing is opening the door ...

Chapter Four: Let's start linking!

The dos and don'ts of linking

Most words are phonetic, i.e. they spell as they sound. 'On', 'get', 'cat' and 'dog' are all phonetic words, so there are no links for them. However, further on you will see links for just under 1000 words that aren't so straightforward to spell, all the way from 'is' to 'accommodation'!

Firstly, here are a dozen dos and don'ts that will help you on your way:

1. If you can't spell the smaller word inside the word then link the smaller word first

For example, the link for 'great' is 'it's gr**eat** to **eat**'. If you can't spell '**eat**' then look up the link for that first. (**E**at **at** the table). Start with the small words then work your way up to the biggies.

2. Shh! Talking is out, now! (Words ending -tion)

The 'tio' part of 'tion' makes the sound 'shh'. So when you hear a word ending with a 'shern' sound then nine out of 10 times it will end 'tion'. Exceptions like 'fashion', 'mission', 'passion' and 'session' are linked further on.

3. Magic 'e' or should that be 'mag ice'?

The magic 'e' rule is: when there's an -e at the end, the vowel says its name.

For example: 'm**a**te', 'P**e**te*', 't**i**me', 'b**o**ne', 'c**u**te'.

So when you hear a vowel say its name, then assume it's spelled that way. The exceptions, of which there are many, are linked in the lists below.

*Very few words end -e*e. So, in this case when you hear 'e' assume it's 'ee', like 'k**ee**p', 'm**ee**t', and 's**ee**k'. Exceptions like 'athlete', 'compete', 'delete', 'scene', 'these' and 'theme' are linked further on.

4. You'd be a fool to put 'full'! (Words ending -ful)

Other than words that are naturally related to the word 'full' like 'overfull' and 'brimfull', all words ending in the sound 'ful' have just one '**l**', i.e 'awfu**l**', 'carefu**l**', 'dreadfu**l**' and 'usefu**l**'.

5. Dis is wrong, Mis! (Words beginning with the prefixes dis- and mis-)

Often people put 'diss' and 'miss' at the start of a word instead of '**dis**' and '**mis**'. So words spelled as 'dissappoint', 'dissapprove' and 'missunderstand' are incorrect. They should be '**dis**appoint', '**dis**approve' and '**mis**understand'

Just remember that 'dis' and 'mis' aren't words. So they have to be attached to another word whereas 'diss' (to insult) and 'miss' can be on their own as they are words in their own right.

6. Could, should and would ... so there! (Words ending -ould)

a) **O U l**iar! If you c**oul**d, you w**oul**d ... and you sh**oul**d!

b) Even though this one makes no sense whatsoever, children tend to like it ... **O U l**ucky **d**uck!

7. Enough, thought, through, rough, tough and though

a) **Ugh**! I haven't th**oug**ht this thro**ugh** en**ough**

b) **O U g**reat **h**erbert! You haven't th**ough**t this thr**ough** en**ough**

c) **O U g**rizzly **h**edgehog! You haven't th**ough**t this road-crossing strategy thr**ough** en**ough**

If you look through the word '**through**', you can see the words tough (thr**ough**) rough (th**rough**) and though (thr**ough**)

8. Leave it out! (Words ending -ely not -ley)

When an adjective ends in '-e', for example 'extreme' and 'definite' then, add '-ly' to make it an adverb.

Most people know this rule but accidentally swap the 'e' and 'l' like this 'extrem**ley**' and 'definit**ley**'. These are, of course, wrong, but the link is easy. Remember to write the city of **Ely** at the end of the adverb 'extrem**ely**' and 'definit**ely**' and you'll get it right.

9. I go hunting tigers (Words ending in -ight)

There are many words that end in the nasty combination 'ight'. I say nasty because the sound they usually make is 'ite'. How these four letters ever arrived together in the same syllable is beyond me but that's why I love the English language, warts an' all!

As the pronunciation is poles apart from its spelling then it's worth using an acrostic.

'**I g**o **h**unting **t**igers' seems to work well with children. So let's give that one a whirl.

Here are ten words that end in 'ight'. (There are more.)

Night   Tight   Bright   Light   Might   Slight   Fright   Sight   Right   Fight

Putting these words into a story, along with the acrostic, will hopefully help you remember their endings.

*If **I g**o **h**unting **t**igers at n**ight**, I need to sit t**ight** with a br**ight** l**ight**. Otherwise I m**ight** get a sl**ight** fr**ight** if I caught s**ight** of one that wants a **right** old f**ight**.*

You may not recall all ten in one go. But reading it a couple more times should do the trick.

10. There, there. It's not your fault. (Their, there, they're, your and you're)

You will see a link accounting for the difference between 'their' and 'there' in the 'Five letter words' section in the linking index. This is useful as these two often get mixed up.

Most children are aware of the spelling of 'your' and that 'they're' and 'you're' are short for 'they are' and 'you are' but just get into bad habits.

Now, this isn't a link but more of a reminder. Before you write down one of these five words, get into the habit of stopping for five seconds and think which one you are saying. Are you saying 'your' or 'you are'? Once you've worked that out, you will spell it correctly nine times out of 10.

Just think ... **Whoa there!**

11. Come off it! (Words beginning com-)

When you hear the sound 'com' at the start of the word, the fourth letter is always a consonant other than 'coma', 'come', 'comedy', 'Comet' and 'comic' all of which have links in the list below. (These are words in everyday use.)

Come to the '**comedy** club' to watch the **comic** rather than drift into a **coma** shopping at **Comet**.

12. Y, oh, Y? (Three letter verbs that have no vowel or contain an 'i' ending with the sound –eye.)

You use '**y**' once and only once, i.e cr**y**/cries and tie/t**y**ing
It's not cr**y**/cr**y**s or tie/tieing

Same goes for these three-letter verbs:

Cry	Dry	Fry	Pry	Shy	Sky	Spy	Try
Cries	Dries	Fries	Pries	Shies	Skies	Spies	Tries

Die	Lie	Tie	Vie
Dying	Lying	Tying	Vying

Key Stage 1: High-frequency words to learn

Remember, phonetic words are not in this list, like 'big', 'but', 'dog', 'dad' and 'from'. A good idea would be to do ten at a time and repeat it a week later. Some links will go 'in' straightaway. Others will take more than one go. If you need a link for the smaller word inside then you will find it in this list or the full list at the end of this chapter.

I can't ask you to remember every single word in one go, so I've split the high-frequency words into bite-sized chunks of 10. Have a go with them and come back later to see if they have stuck.

You can dip into the linking index at the end of this book if you want to find links for other words and there are thousands more on my website www.Thinkalink.co.uk.

GROUP 1: (ABOUT TO BECAUSE)		
TRIED THIS ONE	**CAN REMEMBER IT**	
		About: What are **U** on ab**ou**t?
		After: I prefer to see an **A** not an **F** **af**ter my homework
		Again: a) It's r**ain**ing ag**ain** b) I'm going to watch Lady **Gaga in** concert, **again**
		All: All cars go down **a** road (**ll**)
		Another: a) **Not** an**ot**her one! b) An**o**ther g**o**
		Are: 'a' and 'e' **are** vowels
		As: As you know your **As**, Bs and Cs, you can begin to read.
		Because: a) **B**ig **E**lephants **C**an **A**lways **U**nderstand **S**mall **E**lephants b) … bec**ause a use** for linking is helping you to spell

GROUP 2: (BOY TO DOWN)		
TRIED THIS ONE	**CAN REMEMBER IT**	
		Boy: A boy can be a yob ('**boy**' backwards)
		Brother: a) Yo **bro**! b) **O**, br**o**ther! c) Go **rot**, you smelly br**ot**her.
		Call: We **all call** out once in a while
		Called: We can't **all** be c**alled** 'Ed'.
		Can't: Can it? No it **can't**.
		Come & Some: Some people never c**ome** h**ome**
		Could, Would and Should: O U liar! If you c**oul**d, you w**oul**d … and you sh**oul**d.
		Do and Don't: Don't **do** it, **Don**!
		Door: a) Open your eyes (**o o**) before opening a d**oor** b) Stand behind the d**oor** and say 'B**oo**'!
		Down, Now and Slow: Slow d**own**, n**ow**!

		GROUP 3: (FIRST TO HERE)
TRIED THIS ONE	**CAN REMEMBER IT**	
		First: 1st is in the word f**1**rst
		Girl: Golly! **I** r**e**ally l**i**ke that **girl**
		Go: I've **go**t to **go**
		Going: Oi! Where are you g**oi**ng?
		Good: Oo, that's g**oo**d
		Half: a) **Alf** got h**alf** marks b) **Alf** is h**alf** of **Alf**red
		Has: a) He **has** made a **has**h of this spelling
		Have: You **have** to be**have**
		He, Her & She: Did **he** or s**he** he**l**p **her**?
		Here: a) **He** re**ad here** b) **Here** is **her e**-mail c) Look at **her, he**re!

		GROUP 4: (HIS TO LOVE)
TRIED THIS ONE	CAN REMEMBER IT	
		His, Is and This: This is his
		House & Mouse: Does a mouse in a house use the loo to poo?
		Into: I'm into Tom & Jerry
		Is: Same link as 'his' above
		Last: Last … as always
		Laugh: a) Look at us, giggling happily b) Laugh And U Get Happy c) We have a right laugh in August
		Little: There's only a little left
		Live and Lived: 'Lived live' backwards is 'Evil devil'!
		Look: Look with your eyes (o o)
		Love: I love coming home

		GROUP 5: (MANY TO OR)
TRIED THIS ONE	**CAN REMEMBER IT**	
		Many: Mandy has **many** friends
		Me: Mel me**t** **me**
		More: a) M**ore or l**ess … b) Is it m**OR**e **me** OR you?
		Much: U C mu**c**h better with your eyes open
		Night: I get **h**ome late at n**ight**
		No and Now: No, **no**t **no**w
		Of: Take off the 'f' of '**of**f' to get '**of**'
		Once: Once up**on** a time…
		One: a) **On**e-**on-on**e contest b) A nose has **one** b**one**
		Or: a) Knife **or** for**k**? b) **O, R** you ready **or** what? c) **OR** is an **O**perating **R**oom

		GROUP 6: (OUR TO SHE)
TRIED THIS ONE	**CAN REMEMBER IT**	
		Our: a) **O**f c**our**se **U R** b) **O, U R our** favourite
		Out: Oi **U!** Get **out**!
		People: a) **P**eople **e**mail **o**ther **p**eople **l**ovely **e**mails b) **P**eople **e**at **o**melettes. **P**eople like **e**ggs c) Eskimo **pe**ople live at the North P**ole**
		Pull: P**ull** **up**
		Push: a) Give **us** a p**ush** ... b) Don't p**ush** **us** around!
		Put: a) We p**ut** **up** with parents b) '**Put up**' is the same back to front
		Said: a) **S**ay **a**gain? **I** **d**idn't hear what you **said** b) I **said I** am **sad** inside
		Saw: a) **S**aw **A**nd **W**atched b) **S**aw **w**ood
		School: I get the '**Choo choo**' train to s**chool**
		He: Did **he** or s**he** **he**lp **he**r?

39

		GROUP 7: (SHOULD TO TWO)
TRIED THIS ONE	**CAN REMEMBER IT**	
		Should: **O U l**iar! If you c**oul**d, you w**oul**d ... and you sh**oul**d!
		So: a) I'm **so so**rry b) You're **so so**ft
		Some: **S**ome people never c**ome** h**ome**
		Their and There: **The i** of '**Thei**r' is a person. **The 'r'** of '**Ther**e' is a signpost
		These and Those: a) **The** South East (**SE**) is a compass point b) **These** people call it **the** South East (**SE**). Tho**se** call it the Home Counties
		They: a) T**hey** **help** t**hem** b) **He**, s**he** and t**hey**
		This: **This** is **his**
		To: **To**p **to** t**o**e
		Took: I t**oo**k a l**oo**k with my eyes (**o o**)
		Two: **Tw**ins are **two** people
	TRIED THIS ONE	**CAN REMEMBER IT**

GROUP 8: (US TO WHO)		
TRIED THIS ONE	**CAN REMEMBER IT**	
		Us: a) Don't ru**sh us** b) The **U.S** call **us** 'Brits'
		Very, Eve, Ever and **Every:** 'Every' contains the other 3 words **Ever**y **Ever**y **Every**
		Want: No one w**ants ants** in their pants
		Was: **W**ith **a s**mile
		Water: a) You **ate** wa**ter**? b) I h**ate** wa**ter**, it's so dull c) W**at**er is f**at**-free d) A w**ater r**at
		We and Were: We w**ere we**e, once
		What: W**hat** is that **hat**!?
		When: W**hen** does a **hen** lay an egg?
		Where: W**here**? **Here** or t**here**
		Who: **W**hy is he called 'Dr **W**ho'?

GROUP 9: (WHY TO YOUR)		
TRIED THIS ONE	CAN REMEMBER IT	
		Why: Why is he called 'Dr Who'?
		Would: O U liar! If you could, you would … you should!
		You: a) You Owe Us b) You sounds like U
		Your: U R your own worst enemy

Key Stage 2: High-frequency words to learn

A good idea would be to try out 10 links at a time and repeat them a week later to see if you can recall the correct spellings. Some links will go in straightaway. Others will take more than one go. If you need a link for the smaller word inside then you will find it in this list or the full list at the end of this chapter.

GROUP 1: (ABOVE TO ASK)		
TRIED THIS ONE	**CAN REMEMBER IT**	
		Above: Over and ab**ove**
		Across: Run **across** the road and you will see **a cross** parent
		Almost: 'al' is **al**most a word
		Along and Walk: I took **a l**ong wa**l**k al**ong** the road
		Also: 'Al' is short for 'Alex' but **al**so 'Alison' and' Alan'
		Always: a) There is **al**ways **a l**ong **w**ay to do things and a short way b) Once **a l**inker, **al**ways a linker
		Animal: Animal - **I'm a l**ion
		Any: Andy says **any** spelling can be linked
		Around, Four and Pound: I **O U** around four po**u**nds
		Ask: a) **As**k **as** many questions **as** you wish b) **As**k **a s**illy question...

	GROUP 2: (ASKED TO BOTH)	
TRIED THIS ONE	**CAN REMEMBER IT**	
		Asked: Ask **Ed as** many questions **as** you like
		Baby: Baby sounds like '**Bay B**' with the b & y changed around
		Balloon: Most **ball**oons are **ball**-shaped
		Before: The **Be**ginning is **be**for**e** the **E**nd
		Began: Mum **beg**an to **beg** me to eat my food…
		Being: If we were human **bee**ings we'd be making honey all day!
		Below: Below **w**ater
		Between: It's ok to **bet ween**y amounts **between** friends
		Birthday: Do you remember your **1**st b**i**rthday?
		Both: '**Bot**' and '**Bum**' are **bot**h names for your **bot**tom

		GROUP 3: (BROUGHT TO DURING)
TRIED THIS ONE	**CAN REMEMBER IT**	
		Brought: Who have you **brough**t home, **bro**? **Ugh**!
		Change: Hang on ... where's my c**hang**e?
		Children: Wild ch**ildre**n fill me with **dre**ad
		Clothes: To some people clo**the**s are **THE** most important thing
		Coming: 'Com**i**ng' **omi**ts the 'e'
		Didn't: **I** didn't know that **I** was the only vowel in this word
		Different: **Differ**ent things **differ** ... funnily enough!
		Does and Goes: **D**oes **O**liver **e**at **s**econds? **G**o **o**n, **e**at **s**ome ... more!
		Don't: **Don**'t do it, **Don**
		During: **D**o **U** **ring** your friend **during** supper time?

	GROUP 4: (EARTH TO GOES)	
TRIED THIS ONE	**CAN REMEMBER IT**	
		Earth: a) I've got **ear**th in my **ear** … yuk! b) How on e**art**h can you call that **art**?
		Enough, Thought & Through: a) **Ugh!** I haven't tho**ugh**t this thr**ough** en**ough** b) **O U g**reat **h**erbert! You haven't th**ough**t this thr**ough** en**ough**
		Every: I get excited **eve**ry Christmas **Eve**
		Eye: The word looks like a pair of eyes, a nose and a smiley face eye
		Father: My **fat**her isn't **fat**!
		Following: Follo**wing** a bird with one **wing** makes my head spin
		Found: a) What have **U** found? b) Fo**u**nd **ou**t
		Friend: a) I go to my **fri**end's on **Fri**day b) Man **Fri**day was Robinson Crusoe's **fri**end
		Garden: Let's make a **den** in the gar**den**
		Goes: **D**oes **O**liver **e**at **s**econds? **G**o **o**n **e**at **s**ome … more!

GROUP 5: (GONE TO KNOW)		
TRIED THIS ONE	**CAN REMEMBER IT**	
		Gone: a) It's g**one one** o'clock b) The dog's g**one** to get the b**one** c) It's a g**one**r
		Half: a) **Alf** got h**alf** marks b) **Alf** is h**alf** of **Alf**red
		Head: a) He**a**dache b) **A**head
		Heard: I he**ar**d with my **ear**
		High: a) **G**! **H**ow high? b) How b**ig** and h**igh** is that?
		I'm: **I'm** in love with h**im**
		Important: On holiday it is impor**tan**t to get a sun**tan**
		Jumped: a) I just jum**ped** over a **ped**al bin b) A mo**ped** just jum**ped** the lights c) **Ed** the cow jump**ed** over the moon
		Knew: a) The **K**ing **k**new it all b) I **k**new **K**ate would get **W**illiam in the end!
		Know: a) I don't personally **k**now **K**ate & **W**illiam b) Does Mary **know** that 'Mary **know**' is '**Wonk**y Ram' backwards? c) The **K**ing is such a '**K**now-it-all' d) O**k**, **now** I **know** how to spell it

		GROUP 6: (LADY TO OFTEN)
TRIED THIS ONE	**CAN REMEMBER IT**	
		Lady: a) Lady sounds like **Lay D** with the d & y changed around b) G**lady**s is a **lady's** name
		Leave: I h**ave** to le**ave**
		Light: **I** **g**et **h**ome while it is still **l**i**gh**t
		Magic: Is **Mag** in charge (**i/c**) of the '**Magic** Show'?
		Money: a) M**one**y is number **one** b) I don't **O N E one** m**one**y
		Morning: **G**ood morning
		Mother: a) Go**dmother** b) That is the **moth**er of all **moth**s!
		Near: N**ear** or f**ar** …
		Never: N**ever** open presents on Christmas **Eve**!
		Often: How **often** do you give a link ten out **of ten**?

		GROUP 7: (ONLY TO ROUND)
TRIED THIS ONE	**CAN REMEMBER IT**	
		Only: On**ly on** this occasion ...
		Opened: I o**pe**ned the loo to have a **pee**
		Other: N**ot her**, the **other** girl!
		Our: a) **Of cour**se **U R** b) **O, U R our** favourite.
		Outside: Oi **U**, **Sid**. **Out**side ... now!
		Own: a) Do you **own** a dressing-g**own**? b) We **own** a t**own** house
		Paper: Did you see the picture of that **ape** in the p**ape**r?
		Place: That's an **ace** hiding-pl**ace**!
		Right: Is it **right** if **I** g**o** h**u**nting **t**igers?
		Round: a) I **O U** a r**ou**nd of drinks b) A round-up

	GROUP 8: (SECOND TO STRAIGHT)	
TRIED THIS ONE	**CAN REMEMBER IT**	
		Second: Hold **on** a sec**ond** ...
		Show: **Show** me **how**
		Sister: My si**st**er always comes first (**1st**)
		Small: We were **all** sm**all** once
		Something: a) **Some**thing seems wrong t**o me** b) **Some**thing's up at h**ome** ...
		Sometimes: **Some**times h**ome** sucks!
		Sound: Thu**nd**er sou**nd**s frightening
		Started: You **star**, **Ted**!
		Stopped: We sto**pp**ed the car **2 P**
		Straight: **I** g**o** h**ome** stra**igh**t after school

GROUP 9: (SUCH TO UNTIL)		
TRIED THIS ONE	CAN REMEMBER IT	
		Such: U C such wonderful things
		Suddenly: a) Then su**dd**enly **D**onald **D**uck appeared! b) **Sudd**enly there was a sh**udd**er
		Sure: a) S**ure U R**! b) Are you S**ure U R E**lvis Presley?
		Swimming: a) **M&M**s are swi**mm**ing in calories b) Swi**mm**ing races are often decided by millimetres (**mm**) c) The facilities at this swi**mm**ing pool are mickey mouse (**mm**) d) Do you listen to **Eminem (M&M)** when you're swi**mm**ing?
		Thought and Through: Ugh! I haven't tho**ught** this thr**ough** eno**ugh**
		Today: Day-**to-day**
		Together: To Get Her
		Turn: a) **U**-turn b) **Turn up** to school c) It's yo**ur tur**n
		Turned: U tu**r**ned angry, **Ed** b) It's UR t**UR**n, **Ed**
		Until: Spelling was tricky unti**l l**inking turned up ...

		GROUP 10: (UPON TO WINDOW)
TRIED THIS ONE	**CAN REMEMBER IT**	
		Upon: Put the **c**up **up on** the shelf
		Use: Use the b**us**
		Used: Us, **Ed** and mum **used** Thinkalink!
		Walk: Wa**l**k **al**ong the road
		Walked: Ed wa**l**ked **al**ong the road
		Watch: a) A **w**atchmaker b) **Al**arm **w**atch c) **W**atch the m**atch** d) **A**! **W**atch it!
		While: Worth**while**
		White: Hit the w**hit**e golf ball
		Whole: The **whole w**ide **w**orld
		Window: Close the **window** or else the **wind** ... **ow**!

		GROUP 11: (WITHOUT TO YOUNG)
TRIED THIS ONE	**CAN REMEMBER IT**	
		Without: Without **U**
		Woke: I w**oke** **ok** this morning
		Woken: I was w**oke**n up by a p**oke**
		We're: We're h**ere**
		Word: a) **O** my w**o**rd! b) Say w**o**rds with your mouth **O**-shaped
		Work: H**o**mew**o**rk
		World: The w**o**rld is round (**o**)
		Write: **W**rite **w**ords
		Year: a) A good c**ar** lasts for ye**ars** b) Do your **ears** get bigger over the y**ears**?
		Young: a) Y**o**uth means y**o**ung b) **Yo**ung people say '**Yo**!' c) **Yo**ung people play with **Yo**-Yos

Chapter Five: Linking index - lots of links for lots of words

This is the full list including the above high-frequency words

Two, three and four letter words

Able: Are you ab**le** to stand on one **le**g?

Ace: The 'A**ce**' is a playing-**c**ard

Ache: He**ache**

Aid: First (**1**ˢᵗ) Aid

Air: **I** inhale air

All: **All** cars go down **a** road (**ll**)

A lot (a space between the words): A lot of space

Also: '**Al**' is short for '**Al**ex' but also '**Al**ison' and '**Al**an'

Ante (Before) & Anti (Against): There is an '**E**' in 'B**e**fore' and an '**I**' in 'Aga**i**nst'

Any: **An**dy says **any** spelling can be linked

Arch: An **arc**h has an **arc**

Are: 'a' and 'e' **are** vowels

Area: **Are a** garden and park places you'd find a play-**area**?

As: I've made a h**AS**h of this spelling

Ask: a) **As**k **as** many questions **as** you wish b) **As**k **a s**illy question...

Away: That's **a way away**

Baby: Baby sounds like '**Bay B**' with the b & y changed around

Bait: A fish b**it** the ba**it**

Ball: **All** babies play with a b**all**

Bare: I'm b**a**re in the b**a**th

Bath: Bath mat

Be: **Be** the **be**st

Bear and Bare:
a) B**ears** have **ears** and **are** b**are**-naked
b) Ple**a**se b**ea**r with me

Blew: The wind bl**ew** from **e**ast to **w**est

Blue: Does the Q**ue**en have bl**ue** blood?

Blow: The **w**ind blows

Boat: A boat is **at** sea

Body: With that sort of **bod**, **y** cover it up?

Book, Cook, Look & Took: I t**ook** a l**ook** (**oo**) at the c**ook** b**ook**

Both: a) '**Bot**' and 'Bum' are **bot**h names for your bottom b) **B**oth **of th**em

Bow: a) B**ow** d**ow**n b) A bow and arrow are **w**eap**ow**ns

Boy: A boy can be a yob ('**boy**' backwards)

Bra: Do '**Bra**tz' dolls wear **bra**s?

Busy: A **bus**y **bus**

Buy: **U** b**uy**, I sell

Calm & Placid: **C**alm and pla**c**id

Call: We **all call** out once in a while

Can't: I **can**, you **can**'t

Cast: **C**ast **as**ide

Chef: A **c**hef **c**ooks

Chew: I **ch**ew sweetcorn from **e**ast to **w**est

Clue: There's a cl**ue** in the q**ue**stion...

Coal: The coal fire is **al**ight

Coma: The w**oma**n is in a c**oma**

Comb: **B**rush and com**b**

Come & Some: **Some** people never c**ome** h**ome**

Coop: a) Pigeons '**coo**' in a **coo**p b) There are 2 eggs (**oo**) in the chicken c**oo**p

Coup: What a coup! A real turn-**up** for the books

Crow: A crow has **w**ings

Cute: **Cut**e hair**cut**!

Dawn: I **aw**ake at d**aw**n

Dead:
a) Dead or **a**live
b) Dead **a**ccurate
c) Being de**ad** is b**ad** news
d) Take dead **a**im ...

Deal, Meal and Real: **Ea**t that m**eal** as it's the r**eal** d**eal**!

Debt: a) You get in de**bt** if you **b**et b) A **b**ad deb**t** c) If you're **b**roke, you're in de**bt**

Die: You could **die** if you **di**ve into an empty swimming pool

Do and Don't: **Don**'t **do** it, **Don**!

Does and Goes: Does **O**liver **e**at **s**econds? (**G**o **o**n **e**at **s**ome … more!)

Done: Overd**one**

Door:
a) Open your eyes (**o o**) before opening a d**oo**r
b) Stand behind the d**oo**r and say 'B**oo**'!

Down, Now and Slow: Slow d**own** n**ow**

Dumb: D**umb**bells

Due: Do **U E**mphasise the D of **Due** or do you say 'jue'?

Dude: You're such a **dud**, **dud**e

Duty: Do your **d**uties

Dye: Dye it **ye**llow

Each: a) Do you e**ach** want a Big M**ac**? b) E**ach** child needs to know their **ABC**

Ear: Earache

Earn: Earn money to **ea**t

Easy: Easy **as** that

Eat: Eat at the table

Echo: Does Santa really say '**Ho**, ho, ho' or is that his ec**ho** down the chimney?

Every, Ever, Very and Eve: I get VERY excited e**VE**RY Christmas **Eve**. I never **ever** get bored.

Eye: The word looks like a pair of eyes, a nose and a smiley face

Fast: As **fas**t as that!

Feat: To **eat** a whole chicken is some f**eat**!

Fete: **ET** opening the f**ete** ... are you on another planet?

Film: **F**act. **I** l**ove m**ovies

Find: You **fin**d a **fin** on a shark

Flaw: There's a **flaw** in that **law**

Flow: **W**ater flows

Foam: a) Sh**a**ving foam b) I use shaving fo**am** in the morning (**AM**)

Four: I **O U** f**our** pounds

Foul: Foul-**up**

Fowl: **Fowl**s & **owl**s are birds

Fuel: **F**ill **up e**mpty **l**itres

Full: Full **up**

Gain: 'No pa**in**, no ga**in**' is a say**ing**

Gear: **C**ars have ge**ars**

Girl: **G**olly! **I** r**eally** like that **girl**

Give: a) **I've given** up b) **Give** me **five** minutes ...

Glow: Glow **w**orm

Glue: Super**glue**

Go: I've **go**t to **go**

Gone: a) It's **gone one** o'clock b) The dog's **gone** to get the b**one** c) It's a **gone**r

Good: **Oo**, that's go**od**

Grey and Gray: Gr**e**y (English) & Gr**a**y (**A**merican)

Grow/Grown: Gr**ow**n-ups r**ow**
                   Fl**ow**ers gr**ow**

Hair: a) Love your ha**ir**, s**ir**! b) That is an **A1** ha**ir**style!

Half: a) **Alf** got h**alf** marks b) **Alf** is h**alf** of **Alf**red

Hang and Hung: A m**an** is h**an**ged and a picture is hung

Haul: Haul **up**

Have: You **have** to be**have**

He, Her and She: Did **he** or s**he** h**e**lp **her**?

Head: a) Headache b) Ahead

Heir: He inherits **r**iches

Here: a) **He re**ad **here** b) **Here** is **her e**-mail c) Look at **her**, **her**e!

Hero: A **hero** is a man. Therefore - Him 1 **Her 0**

High: a) **G**! **H**ow hi**gh** b) How b**ig** and hi**gh** is that?

Hose: You normally point a ho**se** south east (**SE**)

Hour: a) **H**our **h**and b) **H**appy **h**our c) Rush **h**our

Huge: A **hug**e **hug**

Ice: Ice-**c**ream

I'm: I'm in love with h**im**

Into: I'm in**to T**om & Jerry

Is, His and This: Th**is is** h**is**

Isle: The **Isle** of Man **is le**ft of England

Isn't: Isn't **sn**ow just great!

It's (it is) and Its (Possession): The apostrophe of it's is a tiny letter i

I've: I've g**ive**n up

Join: Join **in**

Knee & Kneel: Kneel on your **k**nee before the **K**ing

Knew: a) The **K**ing **k**new it all b) I **k**new **K**ate would get **W**illiam in the end!

Know:
a) I don't personally **k**now **K**ate & **W**illiam
b) Does Mary **know** that 'Mary **know**' is '**Wonk**y Ram' backwards?
c) The **K**ing is such a '**K**now-it-all'
d) O**k**, **now I know** how to spell it

Lady:
a) Lady sounds like **Lay D** with the d & y changed around
b) **Glad**ys is a **lad**y's name

Lamb: A lam**b**s says '**B**aaaaaaaa'

Last: Last ... **as** always

Law: '**LA La**w' was an old TV programme based in **L**os **A**ngeles, USA

Lawn: Lawn mower

Lazy:
a) If you know your **A** to **Z**, then **y** are you so l**azy** when it comes to literacy?
b) Lazy sounds like **Lay Z** (Zee) with the z & y changed around

Lead: 'A' leads the alphabet

Leak: Taps leak

Lie: No one likes a lie

Live and Lived: 'Lived live' backwards is 'Evil devil'!

Load, Toad and Road: A load of toads crossed the A-road

Lose: a) You lose an 'o' from loose b) Loss & Lose

Loud and Shout: Shout out loud.

Love: I love coming home

Low: Low down

Made: That made me mad

Mail: a) I love getting mail b) A1 size mail won't go through the letterbox

Main and Britain: The A1 is the mA1n road in BritAIn

Many: Mandy has many friends

Mask: Gas mask

Me: Mel met me

Mean: You're a mean man

Meat: Eat meat

Moan: Man! Do people moan or what?

Monk: The 'o' of 'Monk' is on his bald head

More: a) More or less ... b) Is it mORe me OR you?

Move: Move over

Mow: Try not to mow down whatever is crossing the road

Mr and Mrs: The terms originate from Master and Mistress

Much: U C much better with your eyes open

Nail: Fingernail

Near: Near or far...

New and News: News is new events from the north, east, west and south parts of the world

Nice: Nice ice-cream!

No: No, not now

Nose: A nose points south east (SE)

Numb: a) **Numb**er 1 b) A num**b b**um

Obey: O**bey** and **be**have

Of: Cup **of** c**off**ee

Oh: **O**h, **h**elp!

Once: **On**ce up**on** a time...

One: a) **One-on-one** contest b) A nose has **one b**one

Only: **On**ly **on** this occasion....

Or: a) Knife **or** for**k**? b) **O, R** you ready **or** what? c) **OR** is an **O**perating **R**oom

Ouch: **O**uch! Didn't **U C** me?

Our: a) **O**f c**our**se **U R** b) **O, U R our** fav**our**ite.

Out: **O**i **U**! Get **out**!

Oven: St**ove** and **ove**n

Owe: **We** owe nothing (**o**)

Own: a) Do you **own** a dressing-g**own**? b) We **own** a t**own** house

Pain: You're a p**ain in** the neck

Pair: a) Pair of eyes ('**i**'s)

Paul: **u** are my PAL, PA**u**L

Paw: A bear can make **a W** sign with its p**aw**

Pea: Garden pe**a**

Pear: I **eat** a pe**ar**

Pie: The **Pie**d **Pi**per

Pier: **Pie** & chips on the **pie**r.

Poor:
a) I'm p**oo**r as I have zero, zero (**o o**) money
b) Is **00**7 p**oo**r?
c) **Poo**r people **poo**

Pour: a) Pour into a c**u**p which is **U**-shaped b) Put the **u**mbrella up as it's po**u**ring

Pull: Pull **up**

Pure: **U R** p**u**re class

Push: a) Give **us** a p**us**h ... b) Don't p**us**h **us** around!

Put: 'Put up' is the same back to front

Race: **Car** is in **rac**e backwards

Rail: a) **I** love a r**ai**l journey b) **A 1**st class r**ai**l journey

Rain:
a) R**ain in**doors? Don't be silly!
b) '**Ra**', **in** Egyptian mythology, is the Sun God!

Read: Read by learning your **A**B**C**

Rein: Re**in in** the horse

Rice: Ri**c**e pudding or i**c**e-**c**ream?

Rich: The ri**c**h tend to be in charge (**i/c**)

Roam: Roam **a**bout

Roll: Roll up your br**oll**y

Rose: A rose ar**o**se from the **s**outh

Row: Row a boat in the **w**ater

Rule: If you **r**ule, **U l**ead **e**veryone

Said: a) **S**ay **a**gain? **I d**idn't hear what you **said** b) I **said I** am **sad**

Salt: Would you like **sal**t on your **sal**ad, **Sal**?

Saw: a) **S**aw **A**nd **W**atched b) Saw **w**ood

Says: 'Dad alw**ays** p**ays**' s**ays** mum.

Seat: Take a se**at at** the table

Sew: S**e**w with a n**e**edle

Shoe: Put your t**oes** in your sh**oes**

Show: Sh**ow** me **how**

Sign: Sign your **sign**ature

Sir: I like sir

Snow: a) **Ow**! That sn**ow**ball hurt b) **W**hite snow

So: a) I'm **so so**rry b) You're **so so**ft

Soap: a) Soap and t**ap** water b) Bar of soap c) First so**ap** then t**ap**

Some: a) **S**ome children leave h**ome** b) **So me** and you make two, which is **some**!

Son: a) **S**on and boy b) God**so**n

Sore: Ouch, it's **so re**d!

Soup: Cup-A-Soup

Sow: Sow **o**ats

Such: **U C suc**h wonderful things

Suit: a) **It suit**s **U** b) **U** and **I** are **sui**ted for each other

Sure: a) **S**ure **U R**! b) Are you **S**ure **U R E**lvis Presley?

Swan: A **swa**n **swa**m

Swap: **Swa**p **a**round

Tail: There is a tail (**l**) at the end of the word tai**l**

Talk: **Tal**k **a l**ot

Tea: a) **Tea** bag b) **Ea**t **t**ea at the table

The: 'The' & 'End' both have 3 letters and contain the letter E

They: a) **T**hey **help t**hem b) **He**, s**he** and t**hey**

Tidy: **I'd t**idy **y**our room, if I were you

Tie: It takes **ti**me to **tie** a **tie**

To: **To**p **to to**e

Toe: **Toe**s go from west **to e**ast

Toy: Yot ('**toy**' backwards) sounds like a toy boat

True: I've met the Q**ue**en ... it's tr**ue**!

Tune: **Tu**rn that **tu**ne down! b) That's a st**un**ning tun**e**!

Turn: a) **U**-t**urn** b) **T**urn **up** to school c) It's yo**ur turn**

Two: **Tw**ins are **tw**o people

Tyre: **Y R** ty**r**es rubber?

Upon: Put the c**up up on** the shelf

Us: a) Don't r**ush us** b) The **U.S** call **us** 'Brits'

Use: **Us**e the b**us**

Very: (See 'Eve' above)

View: **V**iew with your **I** from **E**ast to **W**est.

Wait: Wa**it** for **it**, wa**it** for **it** ...

Walk & Along: I took **a l**ong wa**l**k **al**ong the road.

Wand: Wa**v**e a **wa**nd

Want: No one w**ants ants** in their pants

War: Wa**g**e **war**

Ware: Hardware

Warm: a) Getting too warm can harm you b) Warm armchairs are the best!

Was: With a smile

Wash: a) Carwash b) Wash your hands

Wasp: Wasps and asps sting

We & Were: We were wee, once

Weak:
a) Are we a weak nation?
b) You'll become weak if you don't eat your vitamins from E to A

Wear: You wear earmuffs.

What: What is that hat?

When: When does a hen lay an egg?

Whet: Whet the appetite

Whip: Keep your whip on your hip

Who: Why is he called 'Dr Who'?

Why: Why is he called 'Dr Who'?

Woke: I woke ok this morning

Won: I won nothing (o)

Won't: No, I won't. (No is On backwards.)

Word: a) O my word! b) Say words with your mouth which is O-shaped

Work: Homework

Worm: A worm comes out of a hole (o)

Wrap: Wrap up warm

Year: a) A good car lasts for years b) Do your ears get bigger over the years?

You: a) You Owe Us b) You sounds like U

Your: U R your own worst enemy

Five letter words

About: What are **U** on about?

Above: **Over** and ab**ove**

After: I prefer to see an **A** not an **F** af**ter** my homework

Again: a) It's r**ain**ing ag**ain** b) I'm going to watch Lady G**aga in** concert, **again**

Aisle: Aisle **A is le**ft. Aisle B is right

Alien: You didn't see an a**lie**n. Don't **lie**

Along: (See 'Walk' in the 'Four Letter' section)

Aren't: **E** numbers ar**en't** good for you

Argue: You can't argu**e** with how useful **e**-mail is

Arrow: A bow and arrow are **w**eapons

Asked: As**k Ed as** many questions **as** you like

Began: Mum **beg**an to **beg** me to eat my food…

Being: If we were human **bee**ings we'd be making honey all day!

Below: Below **w**ater

Bible:
a) In the **Bible**, I hated the **bi**t where Jesus **ble**d
b) Is '**Le Bib**' a French children's food **bible**?

Blood: Whose b**loo**d is that on the **loo** door?

Board: a) Card**board** b) Boardgame c) Blackboard d) Dartboard

Brain: Your brain **is in** your head

Bread: White **bread** is **bad** for you

Brief: Br**ief** means br**is**k

Broad: **A**broad

Build: Bu**ild**er's **bu**m

Built: A built-**up** area

Canoe: **Can** a t**oe** get stuck in a **canoe**?

Catch: A dog tries to **cat**ch the **cat**

Chasm: A c**has**m is a **h**ole

Chief: Chief **Hi**awatha

Chord: Harpsichord

Chose: I chose those

Class: Who's that lass in your class, son?

Climb: I climbed into bed

Close: Close means Shut (the door)

Cloud: Look up at a cloud

Comet: Do you prefer Comet or Homebase?

Comic: A comic uses a microphone

Comma: Is it Google.com, ma or Google.com?

Cough: Don't hug me with that cough!

Could: O U liar! If you could, you would... and you should!

Cover: Cover over

Cream: a) Salad cream b) Hand cream

Cries: It's a crime if dad cries in public

Crumb: Breadcrumb

Daily: I love you daily

Dairy: a) I run a dairy farm b) A DIY dairy farm sounds fun

Death: a) At death's door b) I love to eat 'Death by Chocolate'

Didn't: I didn't know that I was the only vowel in this word

Doubt:
a) Never doubt a cub scout
b) 'Do U believe, Thomas?' asks Peter
c) Do U doubt BT's phone bills?

Dough/Doughnut: O U Great doughnut!!!

Dozen:
a) Someone called the 12 Apostles the 'Dozy Dozen'. Disgraceful!
b) Do Zen courses last a dozen weeks?

Drama: a) I am a drama queen b) For road dramas, call the AA

Dream: Daydream

Earth:
a) I've got earth in my ear....yuk!
b) How on earth can you call that art?
c) How did life on earth start?

Early: a) 4am is early b) We hear from an early age

Eight: Every evening I get home at eight o'clock

Every, Ever, Very and Eve: I get VERY excited e**VE**RY Christmas **Eve**. I never **ever** get bored.

Fairy: A f**air**y flies in the **air**

Faith: Linking – have fa**it**h in **it**

False: Give me back my fa**lse** eye-lashes or e**lse** ...

Fault: U **l**iar, it was your fau**l**t

Fibre: Eat 'Fruit & Fi**bre**' at **bre**akfast

Field: **Lie** in the fie**l**d

First: **1**st is in the word f**1**rst

Flies: **Fl**ick **fl**ies away from your face

Flood: Don't fl**oo**d the **loo**

Floor:
a) The **loo** fl**oo**r is wet!
b) **00**7 wipes the fl**oo**r with the baddies
c) B**oo**gie on the dance fl**oo**r

Forty: Grandpops sn**or**es when he's having f**or**ty winks

Found: a) What have **U** found? b) F**ou**nd **ou**t

Fraud: A fra**ud** is a d**ud**

Fruit & Juice: **U** and **I** ought to drink fru**it** j**uice** as it has Vitamin **C**

Gauge: It's important to g**aug**e the weather in **Aug**ust as it's holiday season

Ghost: Hol**y** Gho**st**

Giant: **G**reen **g**iant

Glass: My **lass** wears g**lass**es

Gnome: **G**arden **g**nome

Going: **Oi**! Where are you g**oi**ng?

Great: It's gr**eat** to **eat**

Gross: A gr**oss** l**oss**

Group: A pop gro**up** hopes its song goes **up** the charts

Grown: G**row**n-ups **row**

Guard:
a) Keep your guard **up**
b) M**ud**guard
c) Security guard
d) Toothpaste g**u**ards your g**u**ms

Guess: **U** g**u**essed it!

Guide: **U** and **I** need to be gu**i**ded

Heard: I h**ear**d with my **ear**

House & Mouse: Does a mo**use** in a ho**use use** the loo to poo?

Human: **Huma**ns **hum a** tune if they don't know the words

Image: a) Did you see the gross i**mag**e in that **mag**? b) **I'm age** 5 in that **image**

Knife: a) **K**itchen **k**nife b) **K**nife and for**k**

Knock: **K**nock on the **k**itchen door

Laugh:
a) **L**ook **at us**, **g**iggling **h**appily
b) **L**augh **A**nd **U G**et **H**appy
c) We have a right l**aug**h in **Aug**ust

Learn: You l**ear**n by using your **ear**

Leave: I h**ave** to le**ave**

Litre: When my petrol gauge **lit re**d I went to the garage.

Loose: A **loose loo**-s**e**at

Magic: Magic 'e' spells '**Mag Ic**e'

Match: a) I'll see you **at** the m**at**ch b) Wear a h**at** to the m**at**ch

Maybe: It maybe '**maybe**' or '**may be**'

Meant: I **mean**t to be **mean**

Model: a) Rol**e** mod**e**l b) Sup**e**rmod**e**l c) Mod**el El**le Macpherson

Money and Honey:
a) M**one**y is number **one**, h**one**y
b) I don't **O N E** one m**one**y, h**one**y

Month:
a) The m**on**th of **O**ctober
b) 9 m**on**ths **on** and I'm about to have a s**on**
c) M**on**th **on** m**on**th, year on year ...
d) This **mont**h I gave it the Full **Mont**y.

Motor and Cycle: A m**oto**r**c**ycle has 2 wheels (**o o**) and lots of **CC**

Mouth: Sh**ut** your mo**ut**h

Music: Are the **U.S** in charge (**i/c**) of the m**usic** scene?

Naïve: **Evian** (Water) is **naïve** backwards

Never: N**ever** open presents on Christmas **Eve**!

Obese: Ob**ese** people's bellies point East South East (**ESE**)

Ocean: If it was 'Os**ea**n' then it would be a **sea** not an ocean which doesn't make sense!

Occur: **Cr**acks o**cc**ur in old age

Often: How **often** do you give a link ten out **of ten**?

Other: N**ot her**, the **other** girl!

Ought:
a) You o**ugh**t to see yourself in the mirror ... **ugh**!
b) **O, U ought** to **g**o **h**unting **t**igers

Paint: Tin of paint

Paper: Did you see the picture of that **ape** in the p**ape**r?

Patch: a) **Pat Pat**ch the dog b) I've got a **pat**ch on my h**at**

Phase: Has p**has**e 1 been completed yet?

Phone: a) **P**ayphone b) P**h**o**ne ho**me

Peace: P**eace a**nd **c**alm

Piece: A **pie**ce of **pie**

Place: That's an **ace** hiding-pl**ace**!

Plain: In pl**ain** English please ...

Plane: Pla**ne**s **l**a**n**d

Plant: You find an **ant** in a pl**ant**

Pound, Sound, Around: I **O U** ar**ou**nd f**ou**r p**ou**nds. Does that s**ou**nd ab**out** right?

Prior: Prior means Bef**ore**

Prize: No prizes for guessing what the last letter of the alphabet is ...

Puree: Shouldn't it be spelt 'purea' as it's pronounced 'pure A'?

Queue: Join the qu**eue**, if you're from the **EU**

Quiet: A **jet** isn't quie**t**

Raise: Rise is in **R**a**ise**

Ready: a) **Ready**-made b) **Read**y to **read**? c) Ready, **a**im ... fire!

Reign: A new **reign** would **reign**ite the country

Rhino: **R**hinos and **h**ippos

Roast: **R**oast spuds or m**as**h?

Round: a) I **O U** a r**ou**nd of drinks b) A round-**up**

Royal: The Ro**ya**l family say '**ya**'

Saint: Sa**int**s are **in** Heaven

Salad: **A lad** should eat s**alad**

Sauce/Saucer: Why is there **a**n **u**pturned **c**up on my s**auc**er?

Scene: Did you **c** that scary **scene** in the **scien**ce fiction film?

Scent: The s**c**ent of a **c**andle

Seize: Se**ize** the pr**ize**

Siege: People d**ie** in a s**ie**ge

Small: We were **all** sm**all**, once

Sound: I **O U** ar**ou**nd f**ou**r p**ou**nds. Does that s**ou**nd ab**ou**t right?

Speak: A **pea** can't sp**ea**k!

Spell: It's easier to spe**ll** letters between two lines (**ll**)

Steam: A cup of **tea** produces st**ea**m

Story: A sad st**ory** makes me **cry**

Style: 'St**y**le' and 'st**y**' don't exactly go together!

Sugar: Does **sugar** grow in s**u**nny **gar**dens?

Super: That s**upp**er was super!

Swamp: I just **swam** in a **swam**p ... yuk!

Sweat: **A**rmpits swe**at**

Sword: a) A s**word** is a **w**eapon b) Use a s**word** in **war** c) My **word,** what a s**word**!

Table: Tab**le** l**e**g

Teach/Teacher: a) School will te**ach** you your **ABC** b) My te**ac**her loves a Big M**ac**

Tease: Don't te**as**e by offering cream **teas** as they're bad for me

Their and There: The **i** of 'the**i**r' is a person. The '**r**' of '**ther**e' is a signpost.

Theme: The theme today is 'Me'!

These and Those:
a) **The** South East (**SE**) is a compass point
b) **These** people call it **the** South East (**SE**). Tho**se** call it the Home Counties.

Threw: I thr**ew** the ball from **e**ast to **w**est

Thumb: a) **B**roken thum**b** b) **Thumb**elina c) When you put your thum**b** up, the shape it makes with your fist is **b**-shaped

Title: Tie tl' sounds like 'Title' with the e in the middle

Today: Day-**to**-**day**

Total: Go **to** **T**hink-**A**-**L**ink for **total** satisfaction

Touch: Ouch! Don't t**ouch**

Towel: I **owe** you money for that t**owe**l

Train: a) Do you get on or **in** a tra**in**? b) Tra**in**s are a pa**in in** the neck

Treat: We **eat** tr**eat**s

Tries: A con man **tri**es to **tri**ck you.

Until: Spelling was tricky unti**l** **l**inking turned up …

Usage: U sag with little **usag**e of your gym equipment

Using: U sing by **using** your voice

Value: You can't put a valu**e** on the invention of **e**-mail

Vowel: You can't hear the second vow**e**l in this word which is the second vowel in the alphabet … **e**

Waist: 1st rule of fitness - a thin wa**1st**

Wasn't: Wa**sn**'t that **sn**ow just great yesterday!

Watch: a) A **w**atchm**a**ker b) **A**larm w**a**tch c) W**atch** the m**atch** d) **A**! W**a**tch it!

Water: a) You **ate** wa**te**r? b) I h**ate** wa**te**r, it's so dull c) W**a**ter is f**at**-free

Weird:
a) That b**ird** looks we**ird**
b) The 'i before e' rule doesn't apply here. How w**eird**!

Whack: W**h**ack and **h**it

Whale: A w**h**ale is **h**uge

Wheel: Hot W**h**eels

Where: W**h**ere? **H**ere or t**h**ere!

Which: W**h**ich is funnier, a **hic**cup or a burp?

While: Worth**while**

White: Hit the **whit**e golf ball

Whole: The **w**hole **w**ide **w**orld

Witch: Does a **w**i**tch** have an **itch**?

Woken: I was w**oke**n up by a p**oke**

Women/Woman: W**omen** = Zer**o** (**0**) **men**

World: The w**o**rld is round (**o**)

Worse: F**or** better **or** w**or**se ...

Would: a) **O U l**iar! If you c**ou**ld, you w**ou**ld ... and you sh**ou**ld!

Wring: Wring out **w**ater

Wrist: a) **W**ristwatch b) **W**rite **w**ords with your **w**rist

Write: Write **w**ords

Wrong: Wrong **w**ay

Yacht: Being on a y**ach**t gives me a head**ache**

Yearn: I **year**n to wind back the **year**s

Young:
a) **Y**outh means y**o**ung
b) **Yo**ung people say '**Yo**!'
c)**Yo**ung people play with **Yo**-Yos

Youth: Youth means young

Six letter words

Accept:
a) **Acc**ept the consequences if you're caught on **a CC**TV camera
b) **Acc**ept the **acc**usation and get on with it!

Across: Put **a cross** across the thing you don't want

Advice (noun) and Advise (verb): Adv**ice** – '**Ice**' is a noun; Adv**ise** – '**Is**' is a verb

Affect (verb) and Effect (noun): RAVEN: **R**emember - **A**ffect **V**erb. **E**ffect **N**oun
(They can be the other way round but it's rare.)

Afraid: I'd be afra**id** if I were you! b) I'm afra**id I d**id …

Almost: 'al' is **al**most a word

Allege: An **alleg**ation is to **alleg**e something

Always:
a) There is **alw**ays **a l**ong **w**ay to do things and a short way
b) Once **a l**inker, **al**ways a linker

Anchor: a) The **ho**ok of an anc**ho**r b) Spreading An**chor** butter is such a **chor**e

Animal: An**imal** - **I'm a l**ion

Answer:
a) Question: Which Australian state is Sydney in? A**nsw**er: New South Wales (**NSW**)
b) A political m**an swer**ves the **answer**

Around: I **O U** aro**un**d fo**ur** po**un**ds. Does that s**ou**nd ab**out** right?

Ascent: **C**limb the as**c**ent

Assume: Don't assume as it makes an **ass** out of **U** and **me**

August: Look **at U gust** wind, blowing everyone's hats off!

Author:
a) **All U** auth**or**s write a st**or**y
b) **A**y **u**p. The first and last syllables of **Au**thor sound the same but are spelled differently

Autumn:
a) Does **au**tumn begin in **Au**gust and end in November?
b) Are the leaves **all up t**here? **U**m, **m**aybe **n**ot

Barrel: Unload the barre**l**s off the **l**orry, please

Before: The **Be**ginning is **be**fore the End

Bodice: Nice **bod, ice**man!

Bought: What have you just **bough**t, **Bo**? **Ugh**!

Breath: Do you take a br**eat**h before you **eat**?

Bridge and Fridge: Get **rid** of the fr**id**ge over the br**id**ge

Caesar and Caesarean: A&Es **are an** often used place for an emergency c**aesar**ean

Called: We can't **all** be c**alled** 'Ed'

Cancel: **C**an**CEL** **E**very **L**esson … hooray!

Castle: Shall we **cast Les** into the moat?

Casual: Dress as c**asu**al **as U** like

Cement: **C**ement makes **c**oncrete

Centre: The **centre** is the **core**

Cereal: Ri**ce real**ly is the most used **cereal**

Chain: A ch**ain** has l**in**ks

Change: **Hang** on … where's my c**hang**e?

Cheese: **S**melly chee**s**e

Choose: Now close your eyes (**oo**) and ch**oo**se …

Clique: You need a high **IQ** to join a 'geek cl**iqu**e'.

Colour: a) The c**ol**our of **ur** eyes (**o o**) b) The c**ol**our of **ur** cheeks (**o o**)

Comedy:
a) I watch the **Come**dy channel at h**ome**
b) **Come**dy is often about h**ome** truths

Coming: '**Comi**ng' **omi**ts the 'e'

Common: Run **on** the comm**on**

Couple: I **O U ple**nty of favours, not just a **couple**!

County: A county is in a country

Course: **O**f course **U R**

Cousin:
a) The **coins** that our co**USin**s in the US use are 'cents'
b) My **cousin** claims h**ousin**g benefit

Coward: Cow**ard**s don't fight in **war**s

Cuckoo: 'Now **U C** me. Now you don't,' says the cuc**koo**

Defeat(ed): I can't **eat** any more. This meal has def**eat**ed me.

Delete: **Let** me show you where the 'de**let**e' button is …

Desert: a) Desert **s**and b) Desert **s**un c) **S**ahara desert

Design: Who should we **design**ate to do the **design**?

Double: Does Do**uble O** 7 b**le**ed easily?

Dragon: Drag**o**n's smoke ring (**o**)

During: **D**o **U ring** your friend **during** supper time?

Effect: (See 'Affect' above)

Either: Do you pronounce '**Ei**ther' with a long '**e**' or a long '**i**'?

Except: Everyone can **c**ome **exc**ept my '**Ex**'

Excite: **X**mas (**C**hristmas) does ex**c**ite me so

Family: You're fam**ily**, of course **I** **l**ove **y**ou!

Father: My **fa**ther isn't **fat!**

Friend:
a) I go to my **fri**end's on **Fri**day
b) Man **Fri**day was Robinson Crusoe's **fri**end

Fulfil: **Ful Fil** Fal Fel & Fol don't **fulfil** the criteria for a word

Furore: Shouldn't it be spelt 'Furora' as it's pronounced 'Fur Or A'?

Future: **F**reshen **U**p **T**he **U**niverse. **R**ecycle **E**verything

Garage:
a) Go to the g**arage** to find out your c**ar age**
a) G**arag**e mechanics use **a rag**

Garden: Let's make a **den** in the gar**den**

Ground: Und**e**rgr**O**und tunnel (O)

Health: He**al**th and s**af**ety

Heroes: Kiss the feet and t**oes** of your her**oes**

Honest: **H**and on **h**eart, **h**onest

Injury: Is it a 'work **injury**' if you hurt yourself **in jury** service?

Instil: **L**inking insti**l**s confidence

Island: An **island is land** surrounded by water

Knight: A **K**ing's **k**night

Jumped:
a) I just jum**ped** over a **ped**al bin
b) A mo**ped** just jum**ped** the lights
c) **Ed** the cow jump**ed** over the moon

League: **A GU** chocolate pud is in a different le**ague**

Liaise:
a) It's apt that two little people are in the word '**liaise**'
b) To l**iai**se we need to meet **i 2 i.**

Listen: **L**isten **1st** then talk

Little: There's only a litt**le** **le**ft

London: London Zoo

Lonely: **One** person can get l**one**ly

Lovely: It's l**o**vely coming h**o**me

Mature: Look **at U** being all m**atu**re!

Memory: A **memo** is a **memo**ry-aid

Minute: Can you crack a **nut** in one mi**nut**e?

Mirror: Is that a Rolls Royce (**RR**) **or** a Mercedes in the rear-view mi**rr**or?

Monday: B**oo**! It's M**o**nday

Mother: a) God**mo**ther b) That is the **mo**ther of all **moth**s!

Muscle: Mr 'Mus**cle**' - **cle**aning detergent

Notice/Notices/Noticed:
a) Not Ice Not Ices Not Iced
b) Did you not**ice** the **ice**-cream van?
c) Did you not**ice** who was in charge (**i/c**)?

Nought: I scored n**ough**t (**0**) ... **ugh**!

Office: Who's in charge (**i/c**) of this off**ice**?

Opened: I **ope**ned the loo to have a **pee**

Orange: My Or**ang**e mobile phone just **rang**

Outside: Oi **U, Sid**. Out**sid**e ... now!

Palace: a) Does Buckingham P**alace** have **a lace** curtain or two?

Parent: Pa**re**nts **are** always right!

Pencil: Pen**c**il **C**ase

People:
a) **P**eople **e**mail **o**ther **p**eople **l**ovely **e**mails
b) **P**eople **e**at **o**melettes. **P**eople **l**ike **e**ggs

Person: My **son** is a per**son**

Petrol: Petr**ol** and **Oil**

Please: Do **as** you ple**as**e

Planet:
a) You can't fly a **plane** to a **plane**t ... yet!
b) Millions on the pla**net** surf the **Net**

Pocket: Pock**et** s**et**

Police: a) The pol**ice** are in charge (**i/c**) b) Teletubby **Po** has **lice**. Call the **police**

Prince & Princess: Prince Charles and the new Princess Camilla

Priory: I give this pr**10**ry **10** out of 10, Brother John

Pursue: I pursue **U**

Rabbit: **B**ugs **B**unny is a rabbit

Raisin: Do you use self-**raisin**g flour when cooking a **raisin** biscuit?

Rather: I'd **rather rat her** than get in trouble myself.

Really: We **all** really love linking!

Reason: The re**ason** I want **a son** is that I already have 14 daughters!

Recent: If something is re**c**ent it's **c**urrent

Recipe: That re**cipe** was an epic! (**Cipe** backwards.)

Reduce: **Reduc**e your speed when **U C** a **red** light.

Regime: There's always a strict **regime** in an army **regime**nt

Relief/Relieve: **Lie** down to re**lie**ve back pain

Rescue: **U** resc**ue** me

Rhythm: **R**hythm **h**elps **y**our **t**wo **h**ips **m**ove

Rolled: **Ed**, **rolled** up his br**oll**y

Safety: H**ealth** and saf**ety**

Scheme: **He** has a sc**heme** to get **me**

School: I get the '**Choo choo**' train to s**choo**l

Season: ... and in the se**ason** of winter **a son** was born in a manger

Second: Hold **on** a sec**ond** ...

Secret: Come here a **sec** and I'll tell you a **sec**ret ...

Should: a) **O U l**iar! If you c**oul**d, you w**oul**d ... and you sh**oul**d!

Sister: My **sist**er always comes first (**1**st)

Source: So, **U R CE** (Church of England) not Catholic - the **source** of your belief

Spread: Spread **a**bout

Square: **U are** so sq**uare** and dull

Steady: St**eady** l**ad**, st**eady** ...

Stream: a) I **am** in the top str**eam** b) Streams and lakes

Studio: That **stud** in the art **STUDIO** gets a **10** from me!

Subtle: If we're **sub**tle and sneak on a **sub**, then maybe we can win this game. **Le**t's see...

Supply: Who will **supp**ly the ingredients for tonight's **supp**er?

Taught: Teachers rarely t**aught** in **Aug**ust as it's too **hot**

Tenant: I've got **ten ants** in my pants!

Thames: It's such a s**hame** that the **Thame**s is so polluted.

Threat: He is a **real** thr**ea**t

Toilet: Those **tiles** for the t**oile**ts are rubbish!

Tongue: There's **gum on** the side of your T**ON'GUE**' (E is M on its side)

Turned: **U** tu**rned** angry, **Ed** b) It's UR t**UR**n, **Ed**

Unique: Einstein was un**iq**ue and had a seriously high **IQ**

Useful: **L**inking is usefu**l**

Vacuum: Vac**uu**m the BM **double U** please

Walked: **Ed** wa**lk**ed al**o**ng the road

Wander: a) W**a**nder **a**bout b) To me**ander** is to w**ander**

Weapon: a) We**a**pons are **a**rms b) **A**im with your we**a**pon

Window: Close the **window** or else the **wind** ... **ow**!

Wonder/Wonderful:
a) The '7 W**o**nders of the W**o**rld' - which is **O**-shaped
b) **Wo**w, that's **wo**nderful!
c) I w**ond**er what it's like to be James B**ond**?
d) The **Won**derful World of Willy W**on**ka

Seven letter words

Absence: The second S in absence is conspicuous by its absence

Address: You can't **address** the whole school in that m**ad dress**, mum!

Against: I've nothing to **gain** voting a**gain**st you

Alcohol: Did you know there's water in alc**oho**l? An **H** and **2 Os**

Already: Is **Al ready** already?

Amateur: As **a mate U R** a real 'pro'

Another: a) **Not ano**ther one! b) An**o**ther g**o**

Athlete: **Let** me be an ath**let**e, sir...

Attempt (3 Ts and a P): When having a **p**, if at first you don't succeed, **t**ry, **t**ry, **t**ry again.

Awesome: a) **We** are a**we**some b) **E**-mail is aw**e**some! c) **We**sterns are awes**o**me!

Balloon: Most **ball**oons are **ball**-shaped

Battery: A Duracell batt**ery** lasts a v**ery** long time

Because:
a) **B**ig **E**lephants **C**an **A**lways **U**nderstand **S**mall **E**lephants
b) Why does a **case** have a handle? Be**case** you need to carry it

Believe: This is one **lie** you have to be**lie**ve

Benefit:
a) Is there **N E** be**ne**fit to this link?
b) You can see the **be**nefit if you **beef it** up at the gym
c) The ben**e**fits of **e**-mail are endless

Bicycle: Don't ride your b**icy**cle on **icy** roads

Biscuit: a) **Cu**p of tea and a bis**cu**it b) **Cu**stard cream bis**cu**it

Breadth: Your br**ead**th of knowledge will grow if you **read**

Britain: The **A1** is the longest road in Brit**A1**n

Brother: a) Y**o bro**! b) **O**, br**o**ther! c) **Rot** in hell, you smelly br**ot**her!

Brought: Who have you **brough**t home, **bro**? **Ugh**!

Butcher: **But**chers **cut** meat

Caution: Take **caut**ion, if you **C A U**-t**urn**

Chicken: Chicken & **egg**

Clothes: To some, cloth**es** are **THE** most important thing

Collect: I'll **coll**ect you from **coll**ege

College: Once colle**g**e is over, parents need to give you a **leg**-up onto the property ladder (**ll**)

Colonel: Is '**El Colon**' a Spanish book about punctuation?

Column: a) **N**ewspaper colum**n** b) **N**elson's Colum**n**

Comfort/Comfortable:
a) **R** you **able** to get c**om**f**ort**able on the l**oo**?

Compete: Never com**pet**e with the teacher's **pet**

Control: It's **cool** to be in c**o**ntrol

Correct: S**orr**y, that is not c**orr**ect

Couldn't: You could, you nit! ('**Nit** looks like **n't**)

Council: Pe**ncil** me in for the cou**ncil** meeting

Country: A c**o**unty is in a c**o**untry

Courage: As **our age** increases, our c**ourage** grows

Currant: a) Do **Ant** & Dec like curr**ant** buns? b) Curr**a**nts and r**a**isins

Current:
a) Curr**ent** means Pres**ent**
b) **e**-mail is a curr**e**nt form of communication
c) What's the cur**rent rent** please, landlord?
d) If something is rec**ent** it's curr**ent**

Curtain: I can **C U** standing under the c**u**rtain r**ai**l.

Dessert: We're stressed (**desserts** backwards) as our **desserts** haven't arrived!

Dilemma: **D**o **I** l**eave Emma**? That's my **dilemma**

Disease: You could DIE if you get a DI**seas**E on the **seas**

Emperor: Was Emp**ero**r N**ero** a h**ero**?

Evening: Don't **ever** spell it **ever**ning!

Example: I gave my '**ex**' **ample** time to move out

(When you hear the sound 'eggs' at the start of a word, it's normally spelled 'ex' not 'eg' other than **egg**, **ego** and **Egypt.**)

Fashion: Is '**Hi** Fas**hi**on' a magazine?

Foreign: A change of Prime Minister has **reign**ited the Fo**reign** Policy argument

Forfeit: ... and **Fe**derer for**fe**its the match. Murray is Wimbledon champion!

Farther (distance) and Further (time): **Far**ther away. Fu**r**ther y**our** career.
(These definitions are not set in stone but are near enough.)

History: **Hi**, **story**-teller. Tell us a story

Illegal: It's i**ll**egal to park on a double yellow line (**ll**)

Improve:
a) Your spelling will impr**ove ove**r time
b) We need to impr**o**ve on your score of zero (**0**)

Instead: Don't be a b**ad** speller. Be a good one inste**ad**!

January: Did M**ary** have Jesus baptised in Janu**ary**?

Journey: This **e**-book is helping us on **our jour**ney of life

Karaoke: Your Kar**aoke**-singing is **a joke**.

Kitchen: **Hen**'s eggs are in the kitc**hen**

Laundry: Shake out the **undry** la**undry**

Leisure: **I sure** love my le**isure** time

Library: I've left my **bra** in the li**bra**ry … oops!

Licence: You need **2 C** to obtain a Driving Li**c**en**c**e

License: Not licen**sing** your product is a **sin**

Machete: Cutting yourself on a m**ache**te could **ache** a bit!

Marshal: Fie**l**d Marsha**l**

Machine: A **chin**-up for my friend is a breeze … he's a m**achin**e!

Michael: Dr M**ichael** is in charge (**i/c**) at the hospital's (**H**) **A&E**

Minimum: Is a '**mini**' **mum** a small mother?

Miracle: Call the **RAC** for roadside mi**rac**les

Mission: Mi**ssi**on Impo**ssi**ble

Mistake: Make no **mistake**, the **MI5 take** no prisoners

Monarch: Marble **Arch** is near the mon**arch**'s home

Morning: **G**ood morning

Mystery: It's a mystery Y '**Myster Y**' has changed the 'i' of Mister to a 'y'

Natural: **U R A** nat**ural** speller

Neither: Do you pronounce 'N**ei**ther' with a long '**e**' or a long '**i**'?

Nothing: N**o**thing (**0**)

Officer: The offi**c**er is in charge (**i/c**)
Outside: **U**, outside … now!

Passion:

a) **Pass** me the **pass**ion fruit, please
b) On the '**Passio**n' Scale I **pass** with a score of **10**

Patient: You need to be pa**tie**nt to **tie** a **tie**

Penguin:
a) Pi**ngu** is a TV pe**ngu**in
b) **G**, **U in** this country? Surely not, Mr Pen**guin**!

Pharaoh: 'The patron of the Pha**raoh** was the Sun god, **Ra**'…'**Oh**.'

Picture: **Tur**n your head so I can take a pic**tUr**e of U

Plumber: Do you have the pl**umber**'s n**umber**?

Promise:
a) A prom**ise** **is** a prom**ise**
b) I prom**ise** you'll get a pay **rise**
c) The **M15** pro**mis**e to defend the country

Quality:
a) Something that is **A1** is of high qu**A1**ity
b) Muhammad **Ali** was a qu**ali**ty boxer

Quarter: The **Q** for the **art** gallery was a **quart**er of a mile long!

Receipt: Is this piece (**eceip** backwards) of paper the r**eceip**t?

Receive: Yes, yes, **I**'ve rec**eive**d it!

Relieve: **Lie** down to rel**ie**ve back pain

Revenge: R**even**ge is to get **even**

Rhubarb: R**hub**arb is the **hub** of a 'Rhubarb & Custard' pudding…..funnily enough!

Sausage: a) **S**ausage is **a usage** for pork b) **S**outh **A**frica (Boerwoers), **USA** (Hot Dogs) and **Ge**rmany (Frankfurters)

Science: Sci**E**nc**E**-fiction buffs like **2 C** (SEE) Into the future

Session: **5 + 5 = 10**. That ends the maths se**5510**n

Skilful:
a) W**ilf** is sk**ilf**ul
b) Footba**ll** is a skil**ful** game

Soldier: Sol**die**rs **die** in battle

Special: The **CIA** have spe**cia**l agents

Started: You **star, Ted**!

Stopped: We sto**pp**ed the car **2 P**

Success: It's great **2 C** su**cc**ess

Support: I need some **supp**ort cooking this **supp**er

Theatre: a) Going to the the**atre** is **a tre**at b) I'll meet you **there**, AT the **theAT**re

Trouble: **O U** are in so much tr**ou**ble!

Tuesday: Sta**tues**

Twelfth:
a) ... and at the tw**elf**th hour, an **elf** appeared
b) An **elf** appears in the tw**elf**th month of the year

Usually: The bus **U all** catch is **usuall**y late

Village: **I'll age** in this v**illage** as it's so sleepy!

Walking: You'll never see the **King** w**alk**ing **al**ong the road

Weather: a) In the h**eat** of the w**eat**her b) **Eat** outside when it's hot w**eat**her

Welcome: We **l**ove to **cOME** h**OME**

Whether: Whe**ther** **he** likes it or not ...

Whopper: A 'Wh**opp**er' **h**amburger

Without: Without **U**

Woollen: There's a pair of tights (**ll**) in the word 'woo**ll**en' **Wouldn't:** Wouldn't you, you nit? (**Nit** looks like **n't.**)

Eight letter words

Accident:
a) They caught the accident on **CC**TV
b) If, with my 500**cc**, **I dent** a car, it would be an a**cc**ident
c) In **a c**ar **c**rash **I dent** my car
d) **A c**ar **c**rash is an a**cc**ident

Actually:
a) **Actuall**y, **U all act** a bit in life without realising it
b) Act**uall**y, **U all** can link

Apparent: Is it **apparent** that your pa (**ap** backwards) is your **parent**?

Argument: An arg**um**ent over some **gum**? Tut tut

Birthday: Do you remember your **1**ˢᵗ b**irthday**?

Broccoli:
a) Bro**cc**oli - The **2 Cs** are trees and the **l** is the stork
b) Bro**cc**oli has **lots of** Vitamin **C** ... it's **1 L** of a vegetable!

Business:
a) Fido's done his **busin**ess **in** the **bus**
b) There's one S (**ess**) **in** 'bus'
c) I got on a **bus in Ess**ex
d) I got the **bus in** to my place of **busin**ess

Calendar:
a) **Lend a** hand at Christmas (ca**lenda**r)
b) Hertz: We **lend a** CAR for a CA**lenda**R year, at the best rates

Category: People with an **ego** hate to be put into a cat**ego**ry

Children: W**i**ld ch**ild**ren

Complete: **Let** me comp**let**e it for you ...

Corridor: The wallpaper on that c**orri**dor is h**orri**d

Courtesy: Professional tennis players take a **court**esy car to the tennis **court**

Crescent: A crescent is **C**-shaped

Cupboard: Cup Board

Daughter:
a) Was your d**aug**hter born in **Aug**ust?
b) Keep your d**aught**er out of the sun in **Aug**ust as it's **hot**

Decimate: It's **Dec 1, mate,** and your children are about to **decimate** your bank account

Decision: Dec is the **decis**ion-maker in the 'Ant and Dec' partnership

Disaster: The **SAS** try to avert di**sas**ter

Discreet: Be discr**eet** about where we're going to m**eet**

Discrete (Distinct): Dis Crete Island has some distinct features

Emphasis: Cars: Men put too much e**mphas**is on **MPH, as is** their wont

Exercise: Exert energy to lose **c**alories when you **exerc**ise

Exciting: Xmas (**C**hristmas) is so ex**c**iting!

February: R U A sucker for Valentine's in Feb**rua**ry?

Handsome: Han**ds**ome **d**evil

Impostor: 007 is an imp**ost**or

Incision: a) An in**cis**ion **is** a **c**ut b) You see many an in**cis**ion in '**CSI' on** TV

Innocent: In no century is murder an **innocent** crime

Instinct: My inst**inc**t told me I would like 'Monsters **Inc**'

Interest: The **Inter**net has got our **inter**est b) No int**ere**st h**ere**

Lacerate: To la**c**erate is to **c**ut

Language: As **u age**, your grasp of the English lang**uage** improves

Lavatory:
a) Is there **a story** why the lav**atory** chain is broken?
b) Flush **a Tory** policy down the lav**atory**

Literacy & Numeracy: Take care (**erac** backwards) with your lit**erac**y and num**erac**y

Medicine:
a) A **medic in e**mergencies uses **medicine**
b) Clooney was the gorgeous **medic in E**R

Medieval: People did **die** in me**die**val times

Meringue: Does **Pingu** like mer**ingu**es?

Misspelt: I'm **Miss Pelt**, your new English teacher

Nastiest: Sir, **as ties** go, that's the n**asties**t

Nuisance: Nu**isa**nce **is a** nuisance to spell.

Occasion: The **socc**er World Cup is a big o**cc**as**ion (the first o is a football)

Omelette: At h**ome, let Te**rry make the **omelette**

Ordinary:
a) The Virgin M**ary** was no ordin**ary** lady
b) An **A** is no ordin**a**ry grade
c) We live **in a** very ord**ina**ry world

Parallel: There's an **alle**y (ll) in the word 'Par**alle**l'

Pavilion: There's a wicket (lll) in the pav**ili**on

Personal and Personnel: On a pers**onal** note, have you met that **person, Nel**, from '**Personnel**'?

Pharmacy: If you **harm** yourself, go to a p**harm**ac**y** which is **a c**hemist's

Pleasure and Treasure: Discovering tre**asure** is **a sure** ple**asure**

Porridge: That p**orrid**ge was h**orrid**!

Practice (noun) and Practise (verb): Pract**ice** – '**Ice**' is a noun. Pract**ise** – '**Is**' is a verb

Pregnant: My **nan** is preg**nan**t!

Premises: 'Oi, get off my pr**emises**!' yelled Old MacDonald … **e i e** i o

Probably: You're pro**bab**ly being a **baby**

Question: I'm on a **quest** of answering **10 quest10**ns out of 10

Rehearse: My **ears** hurt when loud bands reh**ears**e

Reindeer: **Re**d-nosed **re**indeer

Relevant: Is a navel (**levan** backwards) re**levan**t?

Religion: The **10** Commandments define the relig**10**n of Christianity

Sandwich: Cheese **and** pickle s**and**w**ic**h

Scissors: **C is so** right here, as it's the first letter of 'Cut' (s**cissor**s)

Separate:
a) You sep**arate a rat** from the rest of the class
b) To se**par**ate is to **par**t
c) **Para**graphs se**para**te sentences

Shouldn't: You should, you nit! (**Nit** looks like **n't**)

Solution: **Sol**ve the **sol**ution

Squirrel: Squir**rel**s hate **lor**ries

Suddenly:
a) Then su**dd**enly, **D**onald **D**uck appeared!
b) **Sudde**nly, there was a sh**udde**r!

Surprise: **Burp**!! That s**urp**rised me

Swimming:
a) **M&M**s are swi**mm**ing in calories
b) Swi**mm**ing races are often decided by millimetres (**mm**)
c) The facilities at this swi**mm**ing pool are mickey mouse (**mm**)
d) Do you listen to **Eminem** (**M&M**) when you're swi**mm**ing?

Syllable: There is an L in each syllable of the word syl**la**ble

Thousand:
a) **Us and** 998 others total one tho**usand**
b) **Sand** is made up of thou**sand**s of grains

Together: **To Get Her**

Tomorrow: **Tom Or Row**

Trousers: **Use** a belt with your tro**use**rs

Wardrobe: Ward Robe

Withhold: With hold

Wondrous: The wondrous **Dr** Who

Nine letter words

Architect: 'Arch it a bit more.' says the architect

Admission: Do you have an admission form, Miss?

Assistant: Is Ant Dec's assistant?

Beautiful: Be a beautiful person

Beginning: In the beginning, baby Jesus was born in the inn...

Breakfast:
a) I need breakfast to charge my personal AA batteries
b) Break your fast by eating breakfast

Cardboard: Card Board

Caribbean: Dribbling a football on a Caribbean beach ... heaven!

Champagne: Champagne's too strong for knitting 'Champ' Agnes as she ends up in stitches.

Character: Does my charwoman act like the Queen (ER) or what?

Christmas: Happy Christmas Sam ('mas' backwards)

Chocolate:
a) Chocolate or Coca Cola? Hmm...
b) Chocolate-flavoured Coca Cola? Yuk!
c) You've missed out on the choc, o late one.

Committee: A committee has to hear everything twice (double 'm', 't' and 'e')

Conqueror: Was 'William the Conqueror' a hero?

Consensus: Let's be sensible here and ask what the consensus is ...

Criticise: A critic criticises

Croissant: 'Velcro? Is Santa having a laugh, mum?

Desperate: Desperate measures are taken in an ER (Emergency Room)

Diarrhoea: Runny, runny, help ... oops!

Different: Different things **differ** ... funnily enough!

Difficult: If you join an **iffi 'cult'**, it's d**ifficult** to leave

Disappear and Disappoint:
a) **2 P** or not 2 P? That **S** the question. Shakespeare never di**sapp**oints and will never di**sapp**ear
b) **S**o**pp**y people always di**sapp**oint and need to di**sapp**ear in a flash!
Embarrass/Embarrassing: That's doubly embar**rass**ing, mum!

Favourite: O, U R our favou**r**ite

Following: Following a bird with one **wing** makes my head spin

Happiness: We all **pine** for hap**pine**ss

Important: On holiday it is impor**tan**t to get a sun**tan**

Incubated: In Cuba Ted

Interrupt: Don't int**err**upt Uncle **Terr**y!

Itinerary: These days, it's rare (**erar** backwards) to be given an itin**erar**y

Jewellery:
a) Madame (**Elle**) wears jew**elle**ry
b) I saw some great jewellery advertised in ELLE magazine

Leicester: It can be ice cold in Le**ice**ster

Lightning: In the 100m, Usain '**Lightning**' Bolt may one day break **NINE** seconds (**NINE** letters in '**Lightning**')

Limousine:
a) I'm **usin**g the boss's limo**usin**e ... yippeeeeee!
b) **O, us in** a limo**usin**e ... hello?
d) My c**ousin** has a lim**ousin**e!

Manoeuvre: Man O e U v R e

Medallion: Medal Lion

Miniature: Is a F**iat** Uno a min**iat**ure car?

Minuscule: You score 'A **minus**' for this link, as their is a **minus**cule error

Necessary:
a) It's ne**cess**ary to listen in **c**lass
b) It's ne**C**e**SS**ary to pull your shirt, which has **1 c**ollar and **2 s**leeves, over your left and right **ear**s
c) Playing **C**hess isn't ne**cess**ary

Neighbour: Our n**eigh**bour at number **eigh**t is a right laugh

Orchestra: To play in the or**chest**ra's brass section, you need to have a big **chest** to store those mighty lungs

Panicking: If panicking is your thing are you known as the '**Panic King**'?

Pepperoni: Just **pepper** on **1** and **pepperoni** on the other, please.

Permanent: A lion, with its striking **mane**, is a per**mane**nt threat

Pistachio: Opening pista**chio**s **chi**ps nails

Possesses: Po55e55e5 has **5 Ss**.

Preferred: I **prefer red**

Principal and Principle: Principa(L)eader, Principl(E)thos

Privilege: It's a privi**leg**e just to touch **1 leg** of yours, Mr Beckham

Recommend:
a) I re**comm**end you use **comm**as and full stops
b) I re**comm**end you run on the **comm**on
c) I re**comm**end you read my **commen**ts in your school report

Registrar: Our school regi**str**ar is really **str**ict!

Satellite: Sat**ell**ite **tell**y

Secretary: a) Shh, it's a **secret M**ary b) Shh, it's **a secret**, Miss **Secreta**ry

Something: Some**thing** seems wrong t**o me**

Sometimes: Some**times** h**ome** sucks!

Supersede: Nadal and Djokovic have managed to **superse**DE 'Super' se**ED** Federer

Suspicion/Suspicious: A sus**pec**t looks sus**pic**ious

Vegetable: **Get** the ve**getable**s and put them on the **table**

Wednesday: 'Send' is in the word We**dnes**day, backwards (**dnes**)

Worcester: Feel the **force** of W**orce**ster Sauce!

Xylophone: **X** and **Y** of X**y**lophone make a **Z** sound

Ten letter words

Adolescent: Adole**sc**ent **c**hild

Altogether (completely/entirely): **Salt** is **alt**ogether different to pepper

All together (at the same time):

Funnily enough, 'All together' can be separated, ie 'We did it **all together**' or 'We **all** did it **together**'

Cincinnati: I tan Nic, Nic. (Cincinnati backwards) ... Do you?

Commitment: With co**mmit**ment you can get to the su**mmit** of anything

Definitely:
a) Oops, I'm definitely **in it** now!
b) It's defin**itel**y spelled 'One Tel' not '**1 Tel**'
c) There's a **finite** number of ways to link this word and this is de**finite**ly one of them

Exaggerate:
a) You need to ex**agger**ate to st**agger** me
b) That's not a d**agger**. Don't ex**agger**ate!
c) In the penalty box, footballer **Agger** ex**agger**ates when being tackled

Exhilarate: Hi Lara (Croft), do you find archaeology ex**hilara**ting?

Extinguish: On the TV, did **Pingu** ext**ingu**ish the fire at the zoo?

Fishmonger: Fish**m**o**ng**ers **p**o**ng**

Government: Who does gover**n** the gover**n**ment?

Illiterate: Will it be a problem if I'm **illit**erate?

Irrelevant: A **R**olls **R**oyce, **L**earner plate and **van** ... is this all i**rrelevan**t?

Laboratory: Shall we use a labo**rato**ry **rat or** not?

Lieutenant: Don't **lie, u tenant**. You haven't paid me!

Marvellous: I've got a marve**ll**ous pair of legs (**ll**)

Mayonnaise: Is Double N (Dublin) in County **Mayo**? (**Mayonn**aise)

Millennium: Y2K has **2 Ls**, **2 Ms** & **2 Ns** (Mi**ll**e**nn**ium)

Parliament:
a) My **parent** LIAM is in par**LIAM**ent
b) **I am** in parl**iam**ent
c) I email (**liame** backwards) par**liame**nt but never hear back

Patisserie(s): My favourite Postman **Pat is Series** 1

Permission: Per**miss**ion to go to the loo, **Miss**?

Plagiarise: Liar! You did pla**giar**ise my idea!

Protractor: A '**pro**' **tractor** driver needs to know his angles

Repertoire: Re, Per, To, I, and **Re** ... what a repertoire of small words!

Restaurant:
a) In a resta**urant**, **U rant** at a waiter
b) There's a certain **aura** about rest**aura**nt-owner Gordon Ramsay

Sharpening: Sharp**en**ing a **pen**cil

Silhouette: Take the 's' (for shadow) out of the word '**hou**se' (Sil**houe**tte)

Stationary: a) Station**a**ry? Call the **AA** b) A Station**a**ry c**ar**

Stationery: a) **Toner** is in the word Sta**tione**ry b) **E**-mail is killing off station**e**ry

Veterinary: Is there an **ER in a** vet**erina**ry hospital?

Vocabulary: Babies have a different vocabu**lary**... **la, la, la, la**...

Eleven Letters

Accommodate: I'd love **2 C** if the **O2** Arena could a**ccommo**date all of the world's **M&M**s

Achievement:
a) The achi**eve**ment of man wasn't possible without **Eve**.
b) New Year's **Eve** is a time to reflect on your year's achi**eve**ments

Anniversary:
a) My parents are off to **Double N** (Dublin) for their wedding a**nn**iversary
b) An **ann**iversary is usually an **ann**ual event

Association: The **SS** and **CIA** are spy a**ss**o**cia**tions.

Cappuccino: '**I C cuppa**' is in **C**a**ppucci**no backwards

Caterpillar: **Cater Pillar**

Comfortable:
a) **R** you **able** to get c**o**m**fo**rtable on the l**oo**?

Complement: A **comple**ment **comple**tes something

Compliment: Save the comp**lime**nts, s**lime**-ball!

Counterfeit: Is the second '**e**' in this word a counterf**e**it?

Environment:
a) **Ironmen** triathlons are a high-energy env**ironmen**t
b) There's pressure **on men** and women to create a green envir**onmen**t
c) **N**vir**on**ment

Hallucinate: When you h**alluc**inate, **all U C** are figments of your imagination

Immigration: I**mm**igration is so **M**ickey **M**ouse

Magnificent: What a magnif**ice**nt **ice**-cream!

Maintenance: I give our main**ten**ance man **ten** out of ten.

Millionaire: Millie became a milli**ONAIRe** ON-AIR

Mississippi: Miss is sipping some water

Opportunity: I'll su**pport** you at every o**pport**unity

Persistence: With persis**ten**ce, you'll get **ten** out of ten in your spelling test

Pomegranate: At h**ome, gran ate** p**omegranate**

Reminiscent: Are **recent** MINIS re**MINIScent** of the old style?

Temperature: Temp**era**tures in the modern **era** are rising

Twelve letter words

Abbreviation: **B**&**B** and **BB**C are a**bb**reviations

Acceleration: A motor**c**y**cl**e has serious a**ccel**eration

Accidentally: **Tall** people acciden**tall**y bang their heads

Handkerchief: **Hand**kerchief

Independence: **E**-mail gives you ind**e**pend**e**nce

Onomatopoeia: Old McDonald had a farm, e i **e i a**??? With a quack quack here... (a quack is an OnOmatOpOeia and the four Os correspond to the four letters in farm).

Refrigerator: An ice-cool **ref rig** a match? Never!

Surveillance: I hate surve**ill**ance cameras so much that it makes me feel **ill**!

Taramasalata: tArAmAsAlAtA

Thirteen Letters

Accommodation: (the most commonly misspelled word going)
What are a **C**heshire **C**at, **M**ickey **M**ouse and Scooby **Doo** doing in my acc**omm**od**a**tion?

Accommodation: Our a**cc**o**mm**odation needs **2** **c**ots and **2** **m**attresses as we now have twins

Archaeologist: Archae**o**logist, Indiana Jones' **arch** rivals often ended up in **A**&**E**

Confectionery: Confection**e**ry has **E** numbers

Extraordinary: **Extra Ordinary**

Massachusetts: At **mass**, does **a chu**rch provide **sett**ee**s**?

Mediterranean: Uncle **Terr**y's won a Medi**terr**anean cruise!

Questionnaire: Ladies and gentlemen, we are now approaching **Double N** (Dublin). Could you please fill out the 'Ryan**air**' questio**nnair**e? Thank you.

Fourteen letter words

Correspondence: **e**-mail is the **R**olls **R**oyce of co**rr**espond**e**nce

Uncontrollable: A **roll**ing stone is uncont**roll**able

Add your links to Thinkalink

Well, that just about covers it, for now. There are more than 1200 words linked in this book. However, this is only the beginning as there are many more links out there waiting to be unearthed!

This book is purely about spelling but, don't forget, linking works for learning any fact too, from how many eyes a bee has (five, which rhymes with hive) to what the medical terms are for being knock-kneed (Genu Val**gum**: Does **gum** stick the knees together?) and bow-legged (Genu V**ar**um: Lots of **air** flows through the gap).

My website www.Thinkalink.co.uk is continually evolving as more links are added. So if you want anything linked, anything at all, be it spelling or fact, then submit your request and let's see what the linkers of all shapes and sizes from around the world can come up with. The suggested links can either be cuddled and hugged or swept under the rug. If it's the latter then try and think of your own and submit it. I will then chuck it up the flagpole to see who salutes it (each link is given a mark out of 10 by the public). Who knows, it may even end up in a book one day ...

Linking is subjective. So what works for one person may not work for another. As there is more than one answer, there could be, say, five links for the capital of Sweden being Stockholm. Who cares if it's not a popular one - I just want you to find the links that work for you!

I must just quickly say a huge 'thank you' to those who have submitted links to date. The site is a meeting place online for everyone to share their pearls of wisdom. All I am doing is kick-starting the whole process.

I hope you have enjoyed the ride and, more importantly, grasped the concept of linking and how powerful this underused learning tool can be to aid your child's spelling.

Pip pip!

Sir Linkalot

Sir Linkalot